The Economics
of
Tin Mining in Bolivia

Mahmood Ali Ayub
Hideo Hashimoto

The World Bank
Washington, D.C., U.S.A.

EDITOR	Christine Houle
FIGURES	Pensri Kimpitak
BOOK DESIGN	Christine Houle
COVER DESIGN	George Parakamannil

Library of Congress Cataloging in Publication Data

Ayub, Mahmood Ali, 1948–
    The economics of tin mining in Bolivia.
    Bibliography: p.
    1. Tin Industry—Bolivia. 2. Tin mines and mining—
Bolivia. I. Hashimoto, Hideo, 1937–   II. World
Bank. III. Title.
HD9539.T6B6166 1985   338.2′7453′0984   85–3200
ISBN 0–8213–0514–X

Table of Contents

Preface   *v*

Chapter 1   Introduction and Summary   *3*
    Objectives of the Study   *3*
    Survey for Data Collection   *4*
    Structure of the Study   *4*
    Summary and Conclusions   *5*

Chapter 2   Tin Mining in Bolivia: History and Characteristics   *10*
    The Era of the "Tin Barons"   *10*
    The Nationalization of Large Mines, 1952   *13*
    The Triangular Plan for the Rehabilitation of COMIBOL   *15*
    Recent Tin-Mining and Metallurgical Developments in Bolivia   *18*
    Main Characteristics of Tin Mining in Bolivia   *19*

Chapter 3   The Impact of Tin Mining on the Bolivian Economy   *24*
    Fiscal Results of Tin Revenues   *28*
    Macroeconomic Linkages of Tin Mining   *28*

Chapter 4   Factors Determining Tin Prices and Competitiveness   *30*
    The Demand Curve   *30*
    The Marginal Production Cost Curve   *30*
    Policy Factors   *33*
    Institutional Factors   *39*
    A Review of the World Tin Economy over the Past Decade   *41*

Chapter 5   Problems of COMIBOL   *45*
    Major Problems of COMIBOL   *45*
    Organizational and Management Problems   *46*
    Problems Related to Manpower and Remuneration Policies   *47*
    Lack of Investment   *49*
    Excessive Taxation   *49*
    Heavy Debt Burden   *50*
    Some Recommendations for Changes in COMIBOL   *50*

Chapter 6   Tin Smelting in Bolivia   *55*
    Main Objectives of Tin Smelting in Bolivia   *56*
    Performance of ENAF   *57*

Chapter 7   Issues and Policies Related to Bolivian Mining Taxation   *63*
    Drawbacks of the Present System   *63*
    Alternatives for Mineral Tax Reform   *65*

Chapter 8   Prospects for Tin Mining in Bolivia   67
        International Market Prospects   67
        Domestic Considerations   70

Appendixes
A.   List of Bolivian Mining Companies Included in the Survey   72
B.   Aggregated Sample Data for the Bolivian Tin-Mining Sector   73
C.   Alternative Legal and Contractual Agreements for Mineral Development   74
D.   Problems of La Palca Tin Volatilization Plant   77
E.   Comparative Analysis of Terms and Conditions of Tin Concentrates Contracts   78

Statistical Appendix   79

Bibliography   105

Preface

This study is the result of the authors' work with the Bolivian economy, in general, and with the tin mining sector of that country, in particular. While the focus of the study is on the Bolivian experience, the issues raised are typical of the dilemmas facing economic policymakers in many economies with heavy reliance on a single primary goods sector.

In the preparation of this study, the authors have received invaluable advice and assistance from a number of individuals. The authors are especially indebted to Enrique Lerdau for his continued support of the study. They are grateful to Miss Margaret Joan Anstee, assistant secretary general, Department of Technical Cooperation for Development, United Nations, whose intimate knowledge of the economic history of Bolivia and whose continuing interest in that country contributed considerably. The authors also gratefully acknowledge the comments on a prior draft of Ronald Duncan, Andrew Freyman, Marianne Haug, Arnaldo Leon, Peter Scherer, and Roberto Zagha. The authors are, of course, responsible for all remaining shortcomings.

An important source of background information for the present study was a detailed survey of Bolivia's public and private tin mining sectors. This was ably carried out by a team of Bolivian engineers and economists, including Teresa Alcazar, Gilberto Hurtado and Humberto Zannier. The team received considerable advice on data collection and analysis from Rolando Jordan, chief economist of the Medium Mines Association of Bolivia.

Successive drafts of the study were typed by Anna Maria Galindo de Paz, Adrienne Guerrero, Twain Revell, and Paula Earp. We are thankful to all of them.

Mahmood Ali Ayub
Hideo Hashimoto

The Economics
of
Tin Mining in Bolivia

CHAPTER 1

Introduction and Summary

A caretaker of a Bolivian *finca* (estate) once praised the natural resources of his country to a foreign diplomat. "The whole Cordillera of the Andes is a mass of gold and tin. Here where we stand, we are treading pure gold, and you will sleep tonight on a bed of gold." In relating the anecdote, the diplomat commented, "The man who was walking on gold had no shoes, and his bed was made of mud. In the words of an old philosopher, 'Rich country, poor people.' "[1] Nothing depicts more vividly the bittersweet saga of mining in Bolivia.

From the advent of the Spaniards to Bolivia—then called Upper Peru—in the fourth decade of the sixteenth century, mining has been a mixed blessing for the country. Silver mining led to the elevation of Potosí to the rank of the most populous city in all America by the middle of the seventeenth century. But, the Imperial City was conspicuous because of its glaring contrasts of the big fortunes of the Spanish mine owners and the dire poverty of the indigenous Indian population. It was tin mining that acted as the engine of growth during much of the present century and led to the development of much of the infrastructure that currently exists. And yet there is evidence that at least some of this was achieved at the expense of greater improvements in the working conditions of the mine workers. In short, mining led not only to economic growth but also to social and political polarization of the society. Where tin mining interests—specifically, three major companies (Patiño, Hochschild, and Aramayo), collectively referred to as the "Rosca"—heavily influenced successive governments of Bolivia during the first four decades of this century, there also now exists a trade union movement in the mining sector, which is probably one of the most powerful in Latin America.

In such a charged environment, it is not surprising that few studies have examined the tin mining sector dispassionately from a strictly economic point of view. All too often, writing on the subject has been heavily tainted by the author's ideological outlook. Frequently, data have been distorted or stretched to justify preconceived notions. The present study is an attempt to analyze available data in as objective a manner as possible.

Objectives of the Study

This study has a number of objectives. First, it brings together reliable and consistent data on the sector. Despite the overwhelming importance of tin mining in Bolivia, no systematic efforts have been made, particularly in the public sector, to maintain reliable data. Those who have attempted to analyze Bolivian mining sector data are fully aware of the haphazard nature of the data and the frustrations of developing a consistent time series. Second, most discussions of mining in Bolivia have reviewed only a decade or two of developments. The present study (Chapter 2) analyzes tin mining activities over the past eighty years, for which the authors have compiled production and price data. This long-term view is interesting in assessing the lagged effect of major political upheavals and economic and technical factors, and in obtaining an idea about the future of tin mining in Bolivia. Third, on the basis of the collected information, an attempt has been made to answer such questions as:

How successful was the attempt at rehabilitating the nationalized Bolivian Mining Corporation (Corporación Minera de Bolivia, COMIBOL) during the 1960s? What lessons can be drawn from that experience? What are the main problems of COMIBOL, and what can be done about them? Has tin smelting in Bolivia been a success? What is the macroeconomic impact of tin mining on the Bolivian economy? How competitive in tin production is Bolivia in relation to its Southeast Asian rivals? What are the prospects for Bolivia's tin industry?

Survey for Data Collection

An important component of this study was the estimation of the effect of a change in tin mining revenues on Bolivia's domestic aggregate demand. To achieve this, and to analyze the cost structure of Bolivian tin mining, a survey was carried out for thirteen private mining firms and an equal number of enterprises in the nationalized sector that are either sole producers of tin or produce tin along with other minerals. The sample covered no less than 90 percent of the country's total production of tin. For firms, both private and public, that produce other minerals as well, input costs were carefully prorated. A list of the firms surveyed is provided in Appendix A.

In the course of the survey, detailed information was collected on the use of inputs, production, revenues, taxes, employment, and so on. The survey was completed by extensive interviews with enterprise managers and visits to the mines and smelters. With invaluable support from a team of Bolivian economists and engineers from both the public and private sectors, the data were cross-checked with other sources of information and for internal consistency. The accuracy of the data was checked by computing certain key ratios that ought to be standard across the industry. Such key ratios included total labor costs to total costs, wage costs to total labor costs, total material costs to total costs, and foreign material purchases to total material purchases. Several follow-up visits took place to obtain missing data, to remove inconsistencies, and to find explanations for odd-looking data. In short, every effort was made to ensure the reliability of the data.

Structure of the Study

Chapter 2 provides details about the rise to significance of tin mining in Bolivia, the events leading to the nationalization of the large mines in 1952, and an assessment of the performance of tin mining in the country; it concludes with a description of the principal characteristics of the sector in Bolivia, using the latest available data.

In Chapter 3 an attempt is made to quantify the effect of tin mining on the Bolivian economy. More specifically, the change in the level of domestic aggregate demand resulting from a change in tin output and a change in the international price of tin is measured. There is also some discussion of the fiscal impact of tin revenues and the backward and forward linkages resulting from mining activities.

Chapter 4 contains an analysis of the main factors, economic and institutional, that determine the price of tin. It also includes an assessment of the competitiveness of the various countries and mining methods using data for four benchmark years from 1971 to 1981.

Since its inception in 1952, COMIBOL has been beset by a series of problems, some emanating from its internal organizational structure, others the result of impositions and excessive control by the government. In Chapter 5 an effort has been made to explain why, despite the undeniably high technical caliber of COMIBOL staff since its birth, the corporation has encountered serious problems. The chapter is useful as a case study of the problems a public enterprise can expect to encounter as a result of unclear and even contradictory objectives, too little delegation internally, excessive control from outside, poor signaling systems for management performance, and lack of critical informational flows.

Virtually no study exists that assesses the performance of tin smelting and refining in Bolivia. In Chapter 6, a summary of the most important developments of tin smelting, in both the public and private sectors, is provided. A critical examination of the main objectives for the setting up of tin smelting in Bolivia is carried out, and, on the basis of stated objectives, the technical and financial performance of the State Smelting Company (Empresa Nacional de Fundiciones; ENAF) is analyzed.

One of the main policy constraints on mining development in Bolivia, particularly for private mining, has been the level and structure of mineral taxes. In Chapter 7, the main issues related to Bolivian mining taxation are discussed and recommendations for change are suggested.

Finally, in Chapter 8, prospects for Bolivia's mining and metallurgical activities are studied. Two broad sets of determinants are examined: international factors, over which Bolivia has little or no control; and domestic factors, which can significantly affect the performance of the sector in terms of production and costs.

Summary and Conclusions

The expansion of tin production in Bolivia in the last two decades of the nineteenth century coincided with the rapid decline of silver mining, which had been the basis of the wealth of Bolivia for several centuries. The coming to power in 1899 of the Liberal Party, which was antagonistic to the silver-mining interests, the development of basic infrastructure (particularly railways to the coast) in the first two decades of this century, the increase in demand for tin after the discovery of the vacuum-packed can, and the rise of the automobile industry were some of the factors that aided the growth of tin production in Bolivia. The country's production of tin, which had averaged only 100 tons annually during the 1860s and did not exceed 1,000 tons annually in the 1880s (less than 2 percent of world production) had reached about 24,000 tons by the First World War (amounting to about 20 percent of world production).

The most spectacular period of growth of tin mining in Bolivia occurred in the second half of the 1920s, when production increased by more than 50 percent to a peak of about 47,000 tons in 1929— a level never again reached. The "Rosca," or the oligarchy and the groups of lawyers and others supporting them, were responsible for most of this impressive growth. There is little doubt that tin mining during that era was a lucrative business, aided as it was by a relatively high metal content of ore extracted and a low level of taxation. The fortunes of Patiño, the Bolivian who founded the multinational firm that eventually dominated the world tin industry, are said to have been partly the result of ores of about 50 percent tin content. While this was exceptional, a level of 12–15 percent was not uncommon in 1900; and even in 1925 the metal content of Patiño's Catavi and Siglo XX mines was about 7 percent. By comparison, the metal content of these same mines is currently about 0.3 percent. Mineral taxes as a proportion of total export values remained at about 4 percent during the first two decades of this century, and at about 10 percent during most of the next two decades. By contrast, the figure for 1980 was about 24 percent.

Despite substantial profits, the enclave nature of the mining sector inhibited its direct positive effect on the Bolivian economy. In view of the relatively high capital intensity of the bulk of Bolivian mining activity, factor payments to labor accounted for a small share of total mine revenue. Backward linkages in terms of the use of domestic inputs were virtually nonexistent. Finally, very little reinvestment occurred during the period; foreign-owned companies repatriated most of their funds and nominally Bolivian-owned companies indulged in capital flight. Social conditions in the mines were deplorable, which may, in part, explain the violent nature of the 1952 revolution. Extremely low wages, inadequate housing, and perilous conditions in the mines led to frequent disputes over wages and hours; some of them, as in 1918, 1923, 1942, and 1947, culminated in massacres.

One of the most significant objectives of the revolution of April 9, 1952 was the nationalization of the three largest mining companies, Patiño, Hochschild, and Aramayo. COMIBOL was established to run the nationalized industry.

Over the past thirty years COMIBOL has been considered by many as an unmitigated failure. While the chronic problems of COMIBOL throughout its convulsive history make it difficult to deny this charge, it would be equally difficult to accept the notion that all was well before nationalization and disastrous thereafter. Two factors that predetermined to a large extent the fate of COMIBOL need to be studied: the special circumstances that existed at its birth and the new role perceived for the new corporation by the state.

In the two decades preceding the revolution, a politically unstable environment, the threat of ultimate confiscation, and complicated and unfavorable foreign exchange regulations severely dampened incentives for investment in the country. Private companies withdrew their profits from the country and invested the minimum possible in exploration and development of new ore bodies. Existing shafts were progressively exhausted and mechanization was limited. As a consequence of the neglect of exploration and development, the metal content of tin ores gradually declined.

Other problems, both internal to COMIBOL and external, hampered its operations. The system of *control obrero* (worker control) for the administration of COMIBOL's mines was undoubtedly one. Under the system, union officials were designated for each level in COMIBOL with veto power over the operations of the managers in all matters except "technical." Naturally, all questions ended up being economic, social, or labor-related, with none being exclusively technical. The system had a devastating effect on labor discipline at all levels, the management was subjected to severe pressures by union officials, and absenteeism and disappearance of ore and equipment became all too frequent.

Aggravating the situation was the decision of the government, under union pressure, to rehire the workers discharged for political or health reasons before the revolution. Consequently, the total number of workers employed by COMIBOL increased from 24,000 in 1951 to about 36,500 at the end of 1955; during this period production declined by about 20 percent.

Another important disincentive to production was the administration of the exchange rate. COMIBOL received only 1,200 bolivianos per U.S. dollar for its exports of metal when the market rate was fluctuating between 4,000 bolivianos and 14,000 bolivianos per U.S. dollar. This was essentially a tax on the exports of COMIBOL. At the same time, the government pursued (quite understandably in view of the country's heavy reliance on the mining sector) a diversification policy that siphoned off COMIBOL's surpluses for use in the development of other sectors of the economy, especially tropical agriculture and petroleum. Finally, the international price of tin dropped sharply in 1953–54 because of increased Soviet tin exports and the cessation of stockpiling by the United States of tin and other strategic metals at the end of the Korean War.

Concern about the problems of COMIBOL and more generally about the hyperinflationary situation of the economy, led to the Economic Stabilization Program of 1956. The main macroeconomic components of the program are mentioned in Chapter 2. In the case of COMIBOL, the program also included the elimination of the subsidized company stores (*pulperia barata*) and the reduction of the corporation's payroll by about 20 percent. To complement these measures, the government undertook a comprehensive program of rationalization of the corporation in the early 1960s, referred to as the "Triangular Plan" because it included support from the United States, the Federal Republic of Germany, and the Inter-American Development Bank. The lenders agreed to provide about US$37 million to COMIBOL over a three-year period for exploration, metallurgical research, repairs, and supplies and equipment. The agreement contained provisions prohibiting strikes and limiting the role of labor representatives in the management of the corporation.

Despite the relatively large external financing made available and generous arrangements worked out for bolstering the working capital of COMIBOL, surprisingly little was achieved by the plan. Admittedly, there were some gains—a greater exploration effort, better supplies of food and medicine in the company stores, and the rehabilitation of some mines—but in other areas, achievements were substantially below expectations.

An important objective of the plan—to increase production—was not achieved, and, as can be seen in Chapter 2, the apparent halt in the decline of production reflects only a statistical aberration. Also, despite a decrease in the number of employees, there was no concomitant decline in COMIBOL's current expenditures. There was some improvement in tin recovery in the concentration plants, but this was modest (from 51 percent in 1961 to 54 percent in 1964) compared with expectations. Nor can it be argued that the investment during 1961–64 had a lagged effect, with its impact on production being felt after 1968. This is because the major portion of the investment—some 70 percent—was for emergencies such as immediately needed supplies and equipment, and less than 20 percent was for rehabilitation projects with long gestation periods.

Why was the plan a failure? First, the reduction of the labor force was accompanied by an increase in total labor costs because of a change in the composition of the labor force. More higher-paid surface staff than underground workers were recruited; the percentage of miners working underground declined from 45 percent of the total labor force in 1952 to 33 percent in 1968. Absence of support for the plan from the government, despite its public pronouncements, was another reason. Because of open opposition to the plan from labor, a record number of hours was lost in strikes during the period of the plan. Moreover, the plan was viewed, not only by workers but also by COMIBOL technicians, as having been "imposed." Foreign experts were made directly responsible for operations, no provisions were made for strengthening the internal organization and structure of COMIBOL, and, consequently, when the experts left, there was a complete lack of continuity. To that extent, the Triangular Plan is a good example of how not to execute projects in developing countries.

Performance of COMIBOL over the past decade and its main present problems are highlighted in Chapter 5. Some of these problems may be classified as resulting from its organizational and management structure, its manpower and remuneration policies, lack of investment, excessive taxation, and a heavy debt burden.

Since the nationalization of the large mining companies, the mining industry in Bolivia had been classified into three sectors: COMIBOL, the private medium-size mines, and the private small mines and cooperatives. While there is a legal basis for the distinction between medium and small mines (see Chapter 2), what differentiates a small mining enterprise from a medium one is the scale and type of operation. Small mines typically employ an average of seven or eight people, the operations are rudimentary and labor intensive, and there is a general lack of infrastructure. By contrast, medium-size mines employ an average of about 300 workers and have relatively sophisticated operations. The main problems of the private sector have been lack of credit, particularly over the past five years, as well as inappropriate macroeconomic policies on the exchange rate and mining taxation.

The level of mining taxation in Bolivia has been one of the highest among the major tin-producing countries. In addition, the structure of mining taxation in Bolivia suffers from a number of drawbacks in terms of incentives for efficiency and exploitation. In theory, a move to a true income tax would be desirable. But given the present constraints resulting from a lack of administrative machinery in the Ministry of Finance and the Ministry of Mining and Metallurgy, and the absence of a management and accounting infrastructure in the mining sector itself, it would be advisable to move gradually to that objective. A premature and hurried effort to install a true income tax on the mining sector may be worse than none at all. In Chapter 7, an interim system of taxation based on the indexation of the major inputs is discussed.

Apart from its high level of taxation, Bolivia also has other disadvantages in relation to its main competitors in tin production. The country's mineralized area is essentially confined to rather inaccessible regions of the Andes. Mines are typically located at high altitudes, rendering access to them difficult. Mineral outcrops normally occur in narrow, deep-seated veins, which make mining a high-cost operation. As the analysis in Chapter 4 of Bolivia's export competitiveness in tin production indicates, its production costs (together with those of the United Kingdom) are the highest most of the time, whereas those of Malaysia and Thailand are the lowest. But if these actual costs are adjusted by the degree of overvaluation, Bolivia slips into the middle-cost range, whereas Malaysia and Australia become somewhat higher-cost producers.

Prospects for Bolivia's tin mining and metallurgical activities are expected to be influenced by both international market prospects for tin and domestic performance and policies in the tin sector of the country. Bolivia can exercise relatively little control over the first set of factors except through its membership in the International Tin Council (ITC) and possibly through its influence in the newly created Association of Tin-Producing Countries. By contrast, Bolivia can exercise substantial control over the domestic factors of production, which will be affected primarily by the government's objectives for the sector, plans for the rehabilitation of the nationalized sector, exchange rate and tax policies, and credit availability, particularly from external sources.

The short-term prospects for tin are expected to be influenced primarily by the accumulated stocks, which are at unprecedentedly high levels. Current stock levels are approximately 55 percent higher than the average during the 1970s. It is likely, therefore, that there will continue to be persistent downward pressure on demand for tin in the short term. In the past, producing countries have reacted to such a situation by cutting production so as to maintain their own shares. But, the possibility cannot be ruled out that the ITC system will lose control over markets. In such an eventuality, high-cost producers such as Bolivia will suffer most. Medium- and long-term demand prospects will be affected to a large extent by the degree of substitution from other materials, particularly from aluminum and plastics. As noted in Chapter 8, the relative price of tin with respect to other major metals has increased consistently for at least a century, and if this trend continues, it is bound to affect adversely the future demand for tin. In fact, the use of tin for tinplate production, which constitutes the largest percentage share of tin consumption, has declined over the past decade, partly because of substitution of aluminum and plastics for tin in can-making, and because of technological advances in electrolytic processes, which have reduced the use of tin per square meter of tinplate.

In this context of low growth in the demand for tin, two scenarios are conceivable for the long term. In the first, the current major producers are assumed to continue their control, however feeble, over the world markets. It is assumed that the intervention of the ITC will result in a level of tin prices that would cover the production costs of present producers. In such an eventuality, substitution will continue to proceed in all those activities, such as canning, where such possibilities exist.

In the second scenario, the control over world tin markets of the present producers is gradually loosened by the emergence of new producers. Brazil appears to be the most effective newcomer and may well overtake Bolivia by the late 1980s. If Brazil's expansion stimulates present producers to increase production and to reduce prices, the most likely result could be the ousting of high-cost producers such as Bolivia.

From the domestic point of view, short-term prospects for increased output and improved productivity of Bolivian tin mining are not bright. Past neglect of exploration and mine development, the chaotic situation of COMIBOL, the unresolved status of workers' participation in the nationalized sector, lack of credit, as well as the discouragement of all exporting activities under the present system of exchange rates, are some factors inhibiting recovery. For the private sector, particularly for the medium-size mines, once a proper policy mix (a realistic exchange rate, the adoption of a system of mining taxation that provides more incentives for investment, and greater access to foreign credit) is in place, no other major constraints exist, and capacity utilization can be increased above its present level of about 75 percent. But policy changes alone cannot resolve COMIBOL's problems in the short term. A gradual introduction of the organizational, financial, and administrative changes suggested in Chapter 5 would be needed to put COMIBOL on a sounder financial footing. Many changes can be effected within the present framework of COMIBOL and in the context of the role assigned to the corporation by the government.

Even with a successful rehabilitation program for COMIBOL under way, and with improved international prospects for tin, the problems of public sector tin mining in Bolivia can be expected to persist for several years. Even if some of the more attractive new projects, enumerated later, are executed successfully, the increased production resulting from these investments will be almost completely annulled, at least in the first few years, by declining output of those mines whose deposits have been progressively exhausted.

To summarize, even under the most optimistic scenario, prospects for tin mining in Bolivia appear dim, especially in the public sector. Until the tin potential of the Bolivian lowlands is better evaluated, it may be premature to suggest that the days of tin mining in that country are over. Nevertheless, there is little doubt that the most that can be done in the next few years is to maintain production at its present level. Meanwhile, an effort should be made to diversify gradually not only into other metals, such as gold, silver, and zinc, but also into hydrocarbons and the agricultural and agro-industrial sectors.

Note

1. Quoted by Margaret A. Marsh in *The Bankers in Bolivia: A Study in American Foreign Investment* (New York: AMS Press, 1970).

CHAPTER 2

Tin Mining in Bolivia: History and Characteristics

According to Spanish records, when the Spaniards arrived in Upper Peru—now Bolivia—in 1535, they discovered that the Incas were already operating the mines. Cerro de Potosí, the silver-rich hill that transformed Potosí into the Imperial City, was discovered in 1545. In 1557, near the town of Oruro, then called San Felipe de Austria, the first silver mine started operations.[1] By 1650 Potosí had a population of 120,000. A few years later it reached a peak of 160,000, which made it the most populous city in all of America at that time. The royal city, with its glaring contrasts of the extraordinary wealth of the Spanish mine owners and the dire poverty of the local Indians, declined gradually as the silver mines became exhausted; by 1825, when Bolivia became independent, Potosí's population had been reduced to a mere 8,000. The exhaustion of the main silver deposits was followed during the 1890s by the expansion of tin production, a metal which had hitherto been mined as a by-product of silver. Three important factors aided this expansion. The victory of the Liberal party in 1899 marked a definite shift of power away from the silver-mining interests, still powerful in the Sucre area, to the tin-mining enterprises located mainly in the northern part of the Altiplano.[2] Moreover, in the aftermath of the War of the Pacific with Chile (1879-83), in which Bolivia lost its access to the sea, the first railway connections between Bolivia and the outside world were built. The connection between Oruro and Antofagasta saw the first significant shipment of tin by rail in 1895. This railroad was later extended from Oruro to La Paz and from Oruro to Cochabamba and Potosí. A second major railway connection between La Paz and Arica was completed in 1913. At the same time, world demand for tin started to increase with the discovery of the vacuum-packed can as a means of preserving many types of food, the rise of the automobile industry, and the growing variety of industrial uses of the metal.

Nonetheless, large-scale production of tin has a much shorter history in Bolivia than in the southeast Asian countries.[3] Average annual production during the 1860s was only 100 tons; even in the 1880s, this figure did not exceed 1,000 tons (less than 2 percent of world production). By the end of the century the Bolivian share had risen to 5 percent and was almost 20 percent just before the First World War.

The Era of the "Tin Barons"

The second half of the 1920s witnessed the most spectacular period of growth of the tin industry in Bolivia, with production rising by more than 50 percent—from an average of about 29,000 tons in 1920–24 to a peak of about 47,000 tons in 1929 (see Table 1). Production was severely affected by the ensuing depression, and remained low during the Chaco War with Paraguay (1932-35), which severely drained skilled manpower from the mines.[4] During this period Bolivia continued to have problems meeting its tin quota; its underexport reached 10,000 tons by June 1936.[5] With the end of the Chaco War and heavy U.S. buying during the Second World War, production increased substantially, averaging more than 40,000 tons during 1940–44. The peak level of 1929, however, has never again been reached.

Whereas after Bolivia's independence silver mining was carried out almost exclusively by Bolivian

Table 1. *Bolivian and World Production of Tin Concentrates, 1900–82*
(tons)

| Period | Average annual production | | |
	Bolivia	World[a]	Bolivian production as a percentage of world production
1900–04	11,781	92,800	12.7
1905–09	17,969	102,489	17.5
1910–14	23,460	118,054	19.9
1915–19	25,493	119,274	21.4
1920–24	29,963	119,547	25.1
1925–29	37,764	159,926	23.6
1930–34	25,366	120,965	21.0
1935–39	26,282	174,354	15.1
1940–44	40,096	170,899	23.5
1945–49	37,557	122,434	30.7
1950–54	32,504	171,529	18.9
1955–59	25,218	148,851	16.9
1960–64	22,011	142,458	15.5
1965–69	27,335	172,360	15.9
1970–74	30,780	188,680	16.3
1975–79	31,188	189,320	16.5
1980–82	27,052	197,900	13.7

a. Excluding communist countries' production.
Source: See Statistical Appendix Table 13.

nationals, tin mining attracted a more cosmopolitan group of foreigners as well as some Bolivians; the new companies became complex international ventures directed by professional managers.[6] On the basis of their output and exports, the five most important tin companies in Bolivia during the first two decades of this century were Patiño Mines and Enterprises Consolidated, the Guggenheim's Caracoles Tin Company of Bolivia, Compañía Minera y Agrícola Oploca de Bolivia, Empresa de Estaño Araca, and Compagnie Aramayo de Mines en Bolivie. The major dislocation of the industry in the Depression led to a concentration of production in three major firms: Patiño, Hochschild, and Aramayo. The largest of these, Patiño, was owned by a Bolivian of humble origin, Hochschild was dominated by Mauricio Hochschild, an Austrian who had acquired Argentine citizenship, and the Compagnie Aramayo de Mines en Bolivie was controlled by the Aramayo family, who usually resided in Bolivia but were said to be of Colombian origin.[7] Together, this group of "tin barons" was referred to as the "Rosca," a term designating the oligarchy and the groups of lawyers and others supporting them.[8]

The history of tin mining in Bolivia during this period is interesting not so much for the role of foreign multinationals in that country as for the Bolivian multinational founded by Simon Patiño that dominated the world tin industry. So fascinating is the story of this Bolivian Indian, who, by a single stroke of good fortune, gained possession of the richest vein of tin ore in the world, that it merits a brief description. The story goes that Patiño, then a store clerk in a silver mine in Oruro, gave a prospector credit, accepting as security the prospector's mining claim. The failure of the prospector to pay his debts resulted in the dismissal of Patiño from the company store, leaving him and his wife in possession of the supposedly worthless deeds to the prospector's mines—which, of course, were none other than the valuable tin properties of Llallagua and Uncia. Patiño and his enterprising wife began working the claim almost without help. Later, he made an agreement with the British commercial house Duncan, Fox and Company, whereby they advanced him capital on condition that he sell them his output.[9] A series of acquisitions of French, British, and Chilean

Table 2. *Cost and price comparisons, 1925 and 1981*
(U.S. dollars a pound)

Item	1925	1981
Production costs	0.204	2.913
Transport costs (including c.i.f.)	0.044	0.210
Taxes	0.062	1.007
Smelting and other charges	0.063	2.258
Total costs	0.373	6.388
Average price	0.560	6.390
Total costs as percentage of price	66.6	99.9

companies and his skillful use of credit facilities led to the formation of his group, Patiño Mines and Enterprises, incorporated in Delaware, U.S.A.[10] In addition to his interest in Bolivian tin, banking, and railways, his group acquired control of Europe's largest tin smelter—Williams Harvey of Liverpool—in 1924. The group also acquired partnership in the National Lead Company of the United States, at that time the world's second largest consumer of tin. From then on he was one of the world's wealthiest individuals.

Although detailed data are not available, tin mining in Bolivia during the first four decades of this century was undoubtedly a lucrative business. Data for Patiño Mines and Enterprises for 1925 reveal a total production cost of US$0.37 a pound, at a time when tin was selling at US$0.56 a pound.[11] By comparison, the corresponding tin production cost for the whole mining sector fifty-six years later was US$6.38 a pound, with the international price at about the same level (see Table 2).

These profits were largely the result of the relatively high metal content of ore extracted and the low level of taxation. According to Fox, the fortunes of Patiño derived partly from ores of no less than 47 percent tin content.[12] While this was exceptional, a level of 12–15 percent was not uncommon in 1900. Even in 1925 the metal content of ore in Patiño's Catavi and Siglo XX mines was 6.65 percent.[13] By comparison, the present metal content of these same mines, now nationalized, has fallen to below 0.3 percent.

During this period mineral taxes were typically quite low in relation to both total export values and to profits in the sector. Table 3 provides illustrative data for 1925 for the five largest companies.

Table 3. *Selected Data for the Major Bolivian Mining Companies, 1925*
(U.S. dollars)

Mining company	Taxes paid	Export value	Profits and loss (−)	Taxes paid as percentage of export value	Taxes paid as percentage of profits
Patino Mines and Enterprises	904,604	9,957,756	6,611,219	9.1	13.7
Caracoles	271,303	2,951,888	− 391,583	9.2	n.a.
Oploca	198,081	2,160,150	1,460,088	9.2	13.6
Araca	185,066	2,027,985	885,293	9.1	20.9
Aramayo	159,829	1,740,958	1,139,037	9.2	14.0
Total/average	1,718,883	18,838,737	9,704,054	9.1	17.7

Note: Exchange rates used: US$1 = 2.70 Bolivianos, £1 = US$4.83.
n.a. Not applicable.
Source: Adapted from the table facing page 42 of "Comisión Fiscal Permanente, Tercera Memoria" (La Paz, 1926).

More generally, total taxes as a percentage of total export values remained approximately 4 percent during the first two decades of this century, and about 10 percent during most of the next two decades.[14] By comparison, the figure for 1980 was 24 percent.

Although the mining sector was very profitable, its enclave nature precluded any significant benefits to the rest of the Bolivian economy.[15] Writing in 1927, Marsh referred to this situation: "The mining industry lies, on the whole, outside the general current of Bolivian life, and is largely a foreign enterprise, enriching foreign, or at least nonresident, stockholders—in the heart of Bolivia and yet not in any sense essentially Bolivian."[16] Throughout most of this period, national retained value (defined as the sum of returns accruing to the country from taxes, factor payments, purchase of domestic inputs, and the like) from the sector was minimal. As has already been mentioned, mining taxes as a percentage of export values and of profits were low, except for the period 1936–47 when they averaged about 17 percent. Moreover, in view of the relatively high capital intensity in the bulk of Bolivian mining activity, factor payments to labor accounted for a small share of total mine revenue. Backward linkages in the use of domestic inputs were virtually nonexistent. Finally, very little reinvestment occurred during this period, with foreign-owned firms repatriating their funds on a large scale and nominally Bolivian-owned companies indulging in capital flight.

Deplorable social conditions in the mines may, in part, explain the violent nature of the 1952 revolution. The workers—recruited originally from the Indian peasant population—received extremely low wages, both in relation to wages in other occupations and in relation to prices.[17] Housing was inadequate, and extremely perilous conditions in the mines caused frequent accidents and equally frequent silicosis. In Aramayo's Atocha mill, the Indian workers, men and women, worked twelve hours a day, although more frequently the work day varied between nine and eleven hours.[18] The record for inhuman hours was in a mine near Potosí, where the miners worked on a thirty-six hour shift, taking a little time off at intervals to eat dried corn and chew coca. Marsh refers to some "questionable methods" employed to secure labor. At the time of local feasts, advantage was taken of the "prevailing state of intoxication to bind the Indian to a mine by signing him up and advancing him some pay, which being promptly drunk up, the Indian was forced into the company's debt and had to work in the mine to pay it off."[19]

It was not surprising, therefore, that frequent disputes occurred on wages and hours, some of them (as in 1918, 1923, 1942, and 1947) culminating in massacres.

The Nationalization of the Large Mines, 1952

One of the most significant objectives of the revolution of April 9, 1952, was the nationalization of the three largest mining companies, Patiño, Aramayo, and Hochschild.[20] A commission, in which the Bolivian Mine Workers Federation (Federación Sindical de Trabajadores Mineros de Bolivia, FSTMB) participated, drew up the new law nationalizing the mines. After extensive debate and some unwarranted delays, the law was enacted on October 31, 1952. To run the new nationalized industry, the Bolivian Mining Corporation (Corporación Minera de Bolivia, COMIBOL) was established.

Many writers, Bolivian and foreign, have referred to the history of COMIBOL over the past thirty years of its existence as one of unmitigated failure.[21] Although the chronic problems of COMIBOL throughout its convulsive history make it difficult to deny this charge, it would be equally difficult to accept the notion that all was well before nationalization and disastrous thereafter.[22] Moreover, the special circumstances that existed at its birth and the new role perceived for the new corporation by the state sealed COMIBOL's fate from the moment of the sunrise ceremony at Siglo XX and Catavi commemorating nationalization in 1952.

In the decades immediately preceding the revolution, the politically unstable conditions, foreign exchange regulations, and the threat of ultimate confiscation afforded little incentive for investment in Bolivia. The private mining companies, therefore, withdrew their profits from the country and invested the minimum possible in exploration and development of new sources of ore. No major investment had been undertaken since 1929. According to Gall, the industry "had been sustained for more than twenty years by the efforts of the first three decades of the century."[23] The existing shafts were nearly exhausted and mechanization was limited.

Because exploration and development of new ores had been neglected, the metal content of the ores had progressively declined. Reference has already been made to the high metal content of the ore in the first two decades of this century. According to the Keenleyside study completed just before the revolution, the metal content in Patiño mines was already as low as 1.5 percent by 1950, compared with more than 6.5 percent in the mid-1920s.[24] According to the same report, Bolivian mining was already in a precarious position in 1950.

In addition, other factors hampered the operations of COMIBOL from its inception. These may be broadly classified into those related to, and the outcome of, the general economic and political situation during the 1950s, and those external factors over which Bolivia, let alone COMIBOL, had no control.

The problems of COMIBOL must be set against a background of wider dislocation of national economic activity during the early 1950s and of certain policy decisions adopted by the new regime. Among these policies, the setting up of the system of *control obrero* (worker control) for the administration of COMIBOL's mines was undoubtedly one of the most significant. According to this system, union officials were designated at each management level in COMIBOL with veto power over the operations of the managers in all matters except "technical" ones. Needless to say, all questions turned out to be economic, social, and labor-related, with no problem being exclusively technical. FSTMB was represented at the highest level of COMIBOL. The system of control obrero, together with the euphoria that followed the revolution, had a devastating effect on labor discipline in the mines. The management was subjected to unbearable pressures by the union officials and, in many cases, managers were dismissed by the control obrero. This "lack of discipline" took many other forms: high absenteeism, constant disappearance of ore and equipment, powerlessness of foremen and managers to enforce disciplinary measures, and so on.[25]

Aggravating the situation was the decision of the government, under union pressure, to rehire the workers who had been discharged for political reasons prior to the revolution, as well as those who had been retired for health reasons. As a result, the total number of workers employed by COMIBOL increased from 24,000 in 1951 to about 36,500 at the end of 1955—over a period when production of the corporation declined by about 20 percent. Even Juan Lechin Oquendo, then vice president of the Republic and leader of the mine workers, admitted the adverse effect of this policy on the efficiency of COMIBOL in September 1955.[26]

The administration of the exchange rate proved another disincentive to increased production: when the market rate fluctuated between 4,000 bolivianos and 14,000 bolivianos per U.S. dollar, COMIBOL received only 1,200 bolivianos per U.S. dollar for its export of metals.[27] In effect, this discriminatory exchange rate imposed an implicit tax on the exports of COMIBOL.

The government's policy of economic diversification also affected the performance of COMIBOL. Understandably concerned about excessive reliance on a single primary goods sector, the government siphoned off the surpluses of the corporation for investment in other sectors, especially petroleum and tropical agriculture. This was done either covertly through the discriminatory exchange rate or overtly through lack of investment in COMIBOL.[28]

Apart from these factors which, in one way or another, resulted from government policies, there were others which were the result of external circumstances. To begin with, the price of tin dropped sharply from US$1.20 a pound in 1952 to US$0.91 a pound in 1953, mainly because of increased Soviet tin exports and the cessation of stockpiling by the United States at the end of the Korean War. Moreover, the management problems of the corporation were aggravated by the loss of skilled technicians, both foreign and Bolivian, who left the country to take up jobs abroad with their mining companies. Alexander suggests that the companies even used coercion, threatening their employees with loss of retirement and pension rights if they stayed behind.[29] In addition, although the announcement to nationalize was made on May 31, 1952, nationalization did not take place until October 31, 1952. This five-month delay gave sufficient time to the former owners to repatriate capital, to cut off further exploration, to exploit existing shafts to the maximum, to retain goods in transit in ports in the United States, and Europe or in Antofagasta and Arica, and to remove valuable geological maps from the country. Finally, because of the complex nature of the Bolivian ores and their low metal content, few smelters in the world were equipped to handle the concentrates economically. For several years Bolivian tin had been refined mainly by Williams, Harvey & Company of Liverpool, who reduced smelting costs by combining the Bolivian concentrates with high-content concentrates from East Asia. Patiño owned a substantial interest in Consolidated Tin Smelters, Ltd., which, in turn, owned Williams, Harvey & Company. It is alleged that this monopsonistic position enabled Patiño to hurt the interests of COMIBOL and to collect excessive indemnization for seizure of the mines.

Consequently, production of tin and other metals by COMIBOL declined precipitously during the 1950s. Table 4 provides production indexes for COMIBOL for the major minerals during 1952–60. Tin production declined from about 24,000 tons in 1951 to less than 15,000 tons by 1961.

In view of the problems of COMIBOL and, more generally, the hyperinflationary situation, the Economic Stabilization Program of 1956 was initiated under the presidency of Dr. Hernan Siles Zuazo.[30] The main points of the program, supported by the U.S. government and the International Monetary Fund, were the reduction of the fiscal deficit through a 40 percent reduction of public expenditures and increases in taxes and tariffs; the unification of the exchange rate at 7,500 bolivianos to one U.S. dollar,[31] and the elimination of all exchange, import, and price controls; and the raising of the legal reserve requirement on commercial bank deposits. Measures bearing directly on the problems of COMIBOL were also adopted. These included the reduction of COMIBOL's payroll by more than 7,000 supernumerary workers retrenched with severance pay, the elimination of widespread subsidies on many items,[32] and the replacement of the income and other mineral taxes by a graduated ad valorem export tax (beginning at 10 percent when the price of tin was 90 U.S. cents and rising with any increase in price). This latter measure was meant primarily to increase revenues to the Treasury.

To complement these macroeconomic measures and to rehabilitate COMIBOL, the government undertook a comprehensive program of rationalization of the corporation in the early 1960s; this program was referred to as the Triangular Plan.

The Triangular Plan for the Rehabilitation of COMIBOL

The preoccupation of the government with the deteriorating situation of COMIBOL, together with

Table 4. *Production Trends for Major Minerals of COMIBOL, 1952–60*
(1952 = 100)

Minerals	1952	1954	1956	1958	1960
Tin	100.0	94.5	84.1	63.6	55.7
Zinc	100.0	70.5	83.8	33.1	13.7
Wolfram	100.0	162.7	152.7	54.4	50.0
Lead	100.0	74.6	108.7	76.1	74.0
Copper	100.0	81.9	98.0	56.4	36.1
Silver	100.0	72.9	0.1	0.1	0.1
Gold	100.0	69.1	60.1	42.7	19.1

Source: COMIBOL.

Table 5. *Basic Indicators of COMIBOL Operations, 1959–68*

Indicator	1959	1960	1961	1962	1963	1964	1965	1966	1967	1968
Production (fine metric tons) [a]	15,806	15,230	14,830	15,261	15,393	17,713	16,550	18,420	18,622	18,364
Production (percentage change)	−9.1	−3.6	−2.6	1.0	0.8	15.1	−6.4	11.3	−1.1	−1.4
Labor force	28,622	28,927	28,219	26,843	25,524	25,225	23,072	23,468	22,501	20,917
Underground	9,171	9,477	8,522	8,584	9,358	9,348	8,108	8,167	7,645	6,980
Other	19,451	19,450	19,697	18,259	16,166	15,877	14,964	15,301	14,856	13,937
Direct labor costs [b]	21.6	15.5	17.7	15.7	17.0	19.5	16.4	13.0	13.3	13.3
Indirect labor costs [c]	8.5	8.6	9.9	10.1	10.2	11.0	12.3	13.6	13.6	14.0
Current revenue	42.7	41.8	47.0	45.3	46.1	69.0	78.6	82.3	79.2	79.7
Current expenditure [d]	48.2	40.4	40.4	43.9	42.0	51.0	74.6	77.5	79.3	75.8
Current surplus or deficit (−)	−5.5	1.4	6.6	1.4	4.1	18.0	4.0	4.8	−0.1	3.9
Average price of tin (U.S. dollars a pound) [e]	1.00	1.02	1.13	1.14	1.16	1.58	1.80	1.65	1.48	1.58

a. Includes purchases from "other sources."
b. Includes overtime, compensation for night work, special contract remunerations, as well as altitude, safety, and attendance bonuses.
c. Includes bonuses other than under direct labor costs, social security payments, losses to COMIBOL on subsidized commissaries (*perdida pulperia*) and other social benefits.
d. Including taxes.
e. London Metal Exchange cash.
Source: COMIBOL.

a promise of an offer of US$150 million in aid "without strings" from the U.S.S.R.[33] led to a major Western-supported program for this corporation. In August 1961 a formal contract was signed by the government of the United States, the government of the Federal Republic of Germany, and the Inter-American Development Bank (hence "triangular") as lenders and by COMIBOL as the borrower, with the Central Bank as guarantor. Under this contract, the lenders agreed to advance US$37.75 million to COMIBOL, over a three-year period. The agreement contained several provisions prohibiting strikes and limiting the role of the labor representatives under control obrero. The plan also provided that COMIBOL be exempt from all import duties and export royalties, and that all export taxes paid by the private mines be turned over to COMIBOL to replenish its working capital. It also suspended all indemnity payments to the Patiño, Aramayo, and Hochschild interests until the exact amount of this indemnity could be determined.

Despite the large external financing made available and the generous arrangements worked out for bolstering the working capital of COMIBOL, very little was accomplished by the plan. Admittedly, there were some achievements—a greater exploration effort, a better supply of staples and medicine, and the rehabilitation of some mines, especially the Quechisla and Caracoles group. In other areas, however, achievements were either nonexistent or substantially below expectations.

One of the main objectives of the plan, to increase COMIBOL's production, was not attained. The apparent reversal of the decline in production, which had been evident since 1952 (see Table 5), indicated only that COMIBOL was buying more tin concentrates than usual from "other sources" during this period. These purchased concentrates were counted in COMIBOL's production.[34]

Another important objective not achieved, despite the reduction of staff, was the reduction of COMIBOL's current expenditures (Table 5). Consequently, even with increases in tin prices over the period and despite the relief from tax payments, COMIBOL's current account did not change significantly, except in 1964.

According to World Bank data, tin recovery in the concentration plants was improved from about 51 percent in 1961 to about 54 percent in 1964.[35] This was, however, a modest improvement, especially in relation to expectations.

It has been argued that investment during 1961–64 had a lagged effect on production felt only after 1968. But this hypothesis does not hold true, since the major portion of the investment—some 70 percent—was for immediately needed supplies and equipment. No more than 17 percent of the US$37.75 million invested over this period was for medium- and long-term rehabilitation projects.

Several factors explain the failure of the Triangular Plan. To begin with, although the size of the labor force was reduced from more than 36,500 in 1956 to about 28,000 in 1961 and to about 25,000 in 1964, total labor costs actually increased. The increase was due to a change in the composition of the labor force, with higher-paid above-ground staff increasing in proportion to underground workers: the percentage of miners working underground declined from 45 percent of the total labor force of COMIBOL in 1952 to 33 percent in 1968.

Absence of support for the plan was another critical factor. Despite its public pronouncements, the government was lukewarm to some of the clauses of the agreement, especially those dealing with labor discipline. Only after 1964, under the presidency of General Barrientos, was an unequivocal decision made to limit severely the role of control obrero. Labor openly opposed the plan; because of numerous illegal strikes, particularly during 1961–63, an average of more than 355,000 man-hours was lost each year over the period. The showdown came in June 1965 in the so-called Massacre of San Juan, in which very heavy casualties were sustained.

Equally important, the Plan was viewed, not only by workers but also by COMIBOL technicians, as having been "imposed." Many foreign experts were made directly responsible for operations by being incorporated into the management of COMIBOL. No provisions were made for strengthening the internal organization and structure of COMIBOL or for providing technical assistance and training to local staff. Consequently, foreign technicians were resettled, and when they left there was a complete lack of continuity. From this point of view, the Triangular Plan was a good example of how not to execute projects in developing countries.

Finally, much had been made of improving the metallurgical recovery in the plants. Nevertheless, except for some breakthroughs in flotation, which were applied in Siglo XX, time and money were wasted in a series of dispersed and incoherent investigations abroad that led to no definitive conclusions.

Recent Tin Mining and Metallurgical Developments in Bolivia

The 1970s witnessed a significant recovery in tin mining in Bolivia despite the continuous decline in tin grade over the period and sharp increases in the prices of imported inputs during the first half of the decade. Average production of tin concentrates for the country as a whole exceeded 31,000 tons a year for the period 1970–79, compared with about 25,000 tons during 1960–69 and about 28,000 tons during 1952–59. A number of factors contributed to this situation. The adjustment of the exchange rate in October 1972 from US$1 = 11.88 Bolivian pesos to US$1 = 20 Bolivian pesos clearly had a positive effect on a sector sensitive to changes in the exchange rate. Even the export tax that was levied at the same time to capture some of the windfall profits was not a sufficient deterrent. The improvement of tin prices during most of the decade, but especially during 1973–74 and 1979–80, also increased the incentive for mining those ores hitherto considered uneconomic. At the same time, the country experienced an unprecedented period of stability during 1972–77, marked by a low level of labor strife in the mines. Partly as a result of this stability and partly as a consequence of a euphoria regarding Bolivia's potential as an exporter of petroleum products, the country had ample access to foreign suppliers' credits and commercial loans so that, at least until the end of 1978, credit availability was not a binding constraint on mining development. The value of exports of tin (concentrates and metal) increased almost threefold between 1970 and 1979. Table 6 provides the detailed information and also demonstrates how the country gradually increased its share of exports of metal (rather than of concentrates) after the setting up of the National Smelting Corporation (Empresa Nacional de Fundiciones, ENAF).[36]

Problems in Bolivia's mining sector intensified in 1978. Over the period 1971–77, Bolivia had increased its share in total world tin production from 16.1 to 17.8 percent, 1977 being the year of peak production with more than 33,000 tons of concentrates. Thereafter, however, Bolivia's share declined, falling to only 14.2 percent by 1982. Concomitantly, Bolivia dropped from second largest producer of tin to fourth largest, behind Malaysia, Indonesia, and Thailand.

The pertinent question about the present crisis in Bolivian mining is not why it occurred but what prevented it from happening earlier. The commodity price boom of 1979–80, the devaluation of the Bolivian currency by 25 percent in November 1979, and the elimination of the export tax in early 1980 were some events that postponed the day of reckoning; but these were not sufficient to maintain the momentum of growth in the sector. The severe political instability commencing in 1978, the frequent disruption of production after that year, the deteriorating balance of payments situation of the country, which hampered imports of needed inputs, the precipitous decline in the price of metals after early 1981, and the drying up of foreign credits had a devastating effect on mining operations, both public and private. After 1980 COMIBOL started to register financial losses even on before-tax income.

The exchange rate policy also has had a debilitating effect on mining operations since early 1982. In March 1982 the government instituted a form of dual exchange rates, with 40 percent of all export proceeds being purchased by the Central Bank at the official rate of US$1 = 44 Bolivian pesos, with the possibility of selling the remaining 60 percent on the parallel (free) market. As the divergence between the official and the parallel rates increased, the implicit tax on all export activities increased accordingly. Thus by November of that year, the parallel rate had reached US$1 = 250 Bolivian pesos, whereas the official rate remained fixed at the March 1982 level,

Table 6. *Bolivian Export of Tin Concentrates and Metal, 1970–82*
(US$ millions)

| Year | Tin concentrates | | | | Metallic tin | | | Total |
	COMIBOL	Medium mines	Small mines and coops	Total	ENAF	Other	Total	
1970	64.4	23.3	14.3	102.0	0.0	0.0	0.0	102.0
1971	51.5	17.4	13.1	82.0	23.9	0.0	23.9	105.9
1972	59.2	16.5	13.2	88.9	23.5	1.1	24.6	113.5
1973	67.3	19.3	12.1	98.7	32.3	0.0	32.3	131.0
1974	121.2	28.0	25.3	174.5	55.4	0.2	55.6	230.1
1975	98.2	20.3	11.3	129.8	49.5	0.7	50.2	180.0
1976	113.0	20.3	20.5	153.8	69.3	5.0	74.3	228.1
1977	134.6	21.4	36.9	192.9	131.8	4.1	135.9	328.8
1978	117.0	23.1	32.6	172.7	200.9	0.1	201.0	373.7
1979	95.6	26.8	43.5	167.6	228.0	0.0	228.0	395.6
1980	83.7	15.2	40.4	139.3	238.8	0.0	238.8	378.1
1981	32.8	11.8	32.6	77.2	265.9	0.0	265.9	343.1
1982	20.2	8.9	11.9	41.0	237.3	0.0	237.3	278.3

Sources: Ministry of Mining and Metallurgy; Central Bank of Bolivia.

resulting in an implicit tax of 33 percent.[37] In November 1982 the government unified the exchange rate at US$1 = 200 Bolivian pesos and made it mandatory for all export proceeds to be surrendered to the Central Bank at this rate. Although the parallel market was declared illegal, in the absence of enforcement measures an active market continued to exist, and, moreover, changes in that market rate became the main determinant of domestic (including input) prices.

The exchange rate adjustment considerably enhanced the incentive for exporting. But this improvement was short-lived, lasting only two or three months. A very tight foreign exchange situation and absence of a strong fiscal policy continued to put pressure on the parallel market. Thus by the end of 1983 the parallel rate had reached US$1 = 1400 Bolivian pesos, whereas the official rate (at which all export proceeds had to be surrendered) was moved at the end of the year to US$1 = 500 Bolivian pesos. Needless to say, once again a strong bias was created against export activities, including mining.

Main Characteristics of Tin Mining in Bolivia

Bolivia's mineralized area is essentially confined to rather inaccessible regions of the Andes. Mines are generally located at high altitudes—in some instances above 5,500 meters—and access at times poses formidable infrastructural and logistical problems. Mineral outcrops normally occur in narrow, deep-seated veins, embodied in hard rock, which makes mining in Bolivia a high-cost operation.[38] Furthermore, deposits normally are low grade and frequently consist of complex ores, such as lead-antimony-tin, which can be treated but incur relatively high smelting and refining costs.

Since the nationalization of the large private companies in 1952, the mining industry in Bolivia has been classified into three sectors: the nationalized mining sector (COMIBOL), the private medium-size mines, and the private small mines and cooperatives.

COMIBOL, comprising fifteen large nationalized mines, is the second largest tin enterprise in the world (ranking behind the Indonesian state-owned tin company, P. T. Timah) with average gross sales during 1980–82 of about US$340 million. Of these fifteen mines, only Corocoro and Matilde do not produce any tin (Corocoro produces copper and Matilde produces lead and zinc). Of the remaining thirteen, three (Catavi, Huanuni, and Santa Fe) produce only tin; the others produce tin as well as other minerals.

The medium-size mining sector has consisted in recent years of between twenty-four and twenty-nine private firms, of which two are foreign controlled and five others have varying degrees of minority participation by foreign interests. Of the fifteen medium-size mining companies that mine tin, ten mine only tin. Table 7 presents a summary of the prinicipal characteristics of the sector. The averages in this table conceal a number of features of the firms in this subsector. For example, in 1980 one-third of the firms had gross sales of less than US$1.5 million, whereas three firms had sales in excess of US$12 million. Similarly, while most firms have fewer than 300 employees, at least three firms in 1980 had more than 900 employees.

The rest of the mining sector consists of "small mining" and cooperatives. What differentiates a small mining enterprise from a medium-size one is the scale and type of operation. Small mines typically employ on average seven or eight people, the operations are rudimentary and labor intensive, and infrastructure is generally lacking. Nevertheless, there are at least half a dozen small-scale tin-mining companies in the Oruro and Potosí areas that are larger than some medium-size mining enterprises. The legal basis for the classification is laid down in Supreme Decree 05674 of December 30, 1960. According to this, the main requisites for a private mining company to be classified as a medium-size mining operation are: (1) a minimum level of production, which in the case of tin is 5,500 fine kilos of concentrates a month; (2) a paid-up capital of at least US$100,000, excluding the value of the ores; (3) a minimum of one mining engineer and a financial auditor on a full-time basis; and (4) the company should be registered with the Association of Medium Miners. But in the absence of strict enforcement, classification as a medium-size miner (should the legal requisites be met) depends on the individual mine owner. While there are perceived advantages in being classified as a medium-size miner—better access to credit and the possibility of being able to export directly, instead of being forced by law to sell to the publicly owned Mining Bank (Banco Minero,)—in practice, tax advantages and less exacting accounting requirements encourage the marginal cases to continue as small miners.[39] With one exception, small mines are all locally owned.

In terms of output, the cooperatives make a small contribution, but they account for at least 20 percent of the total mining labor force. There is also a much larger variation in the size of membership, ranging from two or three to more than a thousand. Major tin and silver cooperatives are located in and around the city of Potosí, and several gold mining cooperatives are situated along the Tipuani River.

Table 8 compares the productivity of COMIBOL, the medium-size mines, and the small mines and cooperatives for the period 1973–81. As expected, productivity is highest for the medium-size mines, although, interestingly enough, during the period 1976–78, COMIBOL's productivity equaled that of the medium-size mines, partly because of the tranquil working conditions at that time in COMIBOL's mines compared with much of its history.

Table 7. *Key Average Indicators of the Medium Mining Sector, 1974–80*
(US$ thousands)

Item	1974	1975	1976	1977	1978	1979	1980
Fixed assets	1,325	1,830	2,190	2,410	3,590	4,308	4,816
Sales value	2,625	3,305	3,160	3,895	5,000	7,798	6,692
Profits (after tax)	531	80	535	285	165	163	452
Number of employees	311	298	292	294	336	322	326

Source: Ministry of Mining and Metallurgy.

The working conditions in the mines can be referred to as deplorable, even in comparison with conditions in underground mines of other countries. Health and safety standards in the mines are appallingly low. The pervasive dust from the drilling operations and the absence of adequate ventilation cause a high incidence of silicosis. The average life of a mine worker is thirty-five years. Housing is inadequate, with frequent shortages of water and poor sanitary facilities. It is extremely cold in most mining areas throughout the year, (the tin-producing mine of Caracoles is located just below the snow line). By contrast, inside badly ventilated mines such as Colquiri and Unificada, the temperatures are so unbearably high that the miners have to be hosed down with cold water as they work. Miners take frequent breaks to chew coca leaves, which allegedly dull their pain and appetite but are also considered to be protein rich. In fact, coca leaf is one item that the commissaries dare not run out of.[40]

In this atmosphere of intense physical suffering and isolation, the altiplano Indians have developed over centuries a unique dualistic system of rituals in which Christian ceremonies coexist with those practiced before the Spanish Conquest. Even today, llamas are sometimes sacrificed to Supay or Tio, the Devil Spirit that is supposed to control the wealth of the mines. Miners worship in the chapels and cross themselves before entering the mines, but once inside, names of Christian

Table 8. *Productivity Comparison for Various Tin Subsectors of Bolivia*
(tons of concentrates an employee a year)

Year	COMIBOL	Medium-size mines	Small mines and cooperatives
1973	0.86	1.17	0.08
1974	0.82	0.93	0.08
1975	0.84	0.93	0.12
1976	0.84	0.79	0.08
1977	0.95	0.80	0.09
1978	0.86	0.87	0.06
1979	0.72	0.77	0.06
1980	0.70	0.79	0.05
1981	0.60	0.84	0.06

Source: Ministry of Mining and Metallurgy.

saints are not mentioned for fear of offending the awesome Tio. The famous and colorful Oruro festival perfectly epitomizes this dichotomy. The event is in honor of the Virgin of Socavon (Virgin of the mine mouth). Most of the week is taken up with events depicting ancient traditions and myths, culminating in the grand procession on Saturday of dancers dressed as devils, condors, temptresses, and the like. On Sunday, the masqueraders reveal themselves in front of the Church of the Virgin de Socavon.

Despite some improvements in medical services in the mines, *yatiris* or herbal curers, have a large clientele. As in many Asian and African countries, some individuals are supposed to have *bankanowi* or evil eye, and they are avoided as much as possible.

Notes

1. Alberto Crespo Rodas, "Fundación de la Villa de San Felipe de Austria", *Revista Historica*, vol. 29 (La Paz, 1967).

2. Robert J. Alexander, *Bolivia: Past, Present and Future of Its Politics* (New York: Praeger, 1982).

3. William Robertson, *Tin: Its Production and Marketing* (Westport, Conn.: Greenwood Press, 1982).

4. The bitter fighting on the southeastern frontier left 100,000 Bolivian men dead, wounded, deserted, or captured. During this period, some 4,000 women were employed in the mines. See June Nash, *We Eat the Mines and*

the Mines Eat Us: Dependency and Exploitation in Bolivian Tin Mines (New York: Columbia University Press, 1979).

5. William Fox, *Tin: The Working of a Commodity Agreement* (London: Mining Journal Books Limited, 1974).

6. Jerry Ladman, ed., *Modern-Day Bolivia: Legacy of the Revolution and Prospects for the Future* (Tempe, Ariz.: Arizona State University, 1982).

7. Alexander, *Bolivia: Past, Present and Future of its Politics.*

8. For a description of the life and times of these mine owners see: H. S. Klein, "The Creation of the Patiño Tin Empire," *Inter-American Economic Affairs*, autumn, 1965; C. F. Geddes, *Patino, the Tin King* (London: Robert Hale, 1972); Sergio Almaraz Paz, *El Poder y La Caida* (La Paz: Editorial Los Amigos del Libro, 1980); Alfonso Crespo, *Los Aramayo de Chichas: Tres Generaciones de Mineros Bolivianos* (Barcelona: Editorial Blume, 1981); and Roberto Querejasu Calvo, *Llallagua: Historia de Una Montaña* (La Paz: Editorial Los Amigos del Libro, 1977).

9. New York Times (December 22, 1926).

10. C. F. Geddes, *Patiño, the Tin King* (London: Robert Hale, 1972).

11. Patiño Mines and Enterprises Consolidated, *Annual Report*, December 31, 1925 (La Paz, Bolivia).

12. David J. Fox, "The Bolivian Tin Mining Industry: Some Geographical and Economic Problems," in ITC, *Proceedings of a Technical Conference on Tin* (London, 1967).

13. Walter Gomez D'Angelo, "Mining in the Economic Development of Bolivia," Ph.D. dissertation (Nashville: Vanderbilt University, 1973).

14. Gillis and others provide a figure of 1.5 percent for 1921, but this is not borne out by data. See Malcolm Gillis, *Taxation and Mining: Non-fuel Minerals in Bolivia and Other Countries* (Cambridge, Mass.: Ballinger Publishing Company, 1978).

15. For a detailed analysis of the effect of tin mining on the present Bolivian economy, see Chapter 3.

16. Margaret Marsh, *The Bankers in Bolivia: A Study in American Foreign Investment* (New York: AMS Press, 1970).

17. For evidence, see Manuel Eduardo Contreras, "Tin Mining in Bolivia, 1900-1925." Unpublished M.A. dissertation, University of London, September 1980.

18. W. L. Schurz, *Bolivia: A Commercial and Industrial Handbook.*

19. Margaret Marsh, *The Bankers in Bolivia: A Study in American Foreign Investment* (New York: AMS Press, 1970).

20. The other objectives were land reform, universal voting rights, labor participation in management of the nationalized mines, and dissolution of the army.

21. See, for example, Alberto Ostria Gutierrez, *A People Crucified: The Tragedy of Bolivia* (New York: Prestige Book, 1958) and Cornelius H. Zondag, *The Bolivian Economy, 1952–65: The Revolution and Its Aftermath* (New York: Praeger, 1966).

22. For a detailed discussion of the present problems of COMIBOL, see Chapter 5.

23. Norman Gall, "Bolivia: The Price of Tin. Part II: The Crisis of Nationalization." The American Universities Field Staff Report (Washington, D.C.), vol. 21, no. 2, 1974.

24. Hugh Keenleyside, *Report of the United Nations Mission of Technical Assistance to Bolivia* (New York: United Nations, 1951).

25. Hillman, by contrast, argues that technical and economic factors were much more important than lack of discipline and other social problems during the first few years of the existence of COMIBOL. See John Hillman, "The Nationalized Mining Industry of Bolivia, 1952–1956" (processed, 1982). In the opinion of the present authors, Hillman's interpretation errs on the other extreme, that is, that COMIBOL had no responsibility at all for the deteriorating situation.

26. Quoted in Amado Canelas Orellana: *¿Quiebra de la Mineria Estatal Boliviana?* (La Paz: Los Amigos del Libro, 1981).

27. There was in fact a complicated maze of multiple exchange rates including the official rate of 190, the rate for COMIBOL of 1,200, the rate to the State Petroleum Company (YPFB) of 1,500, and the rate paid for meat imports of 560 bolivianos to one U.S. dollar.

28. Total investment in COMIBOL throughout the 1950s was only US$3 million, for a company whose annual gross exports over the period exceeded US$60 million.

29. Alexander, *Bolivia: Past, Present and Future of its Politics.*

30. For an interesting and intimate account by one who headed the formulation of the program, see George Jackson Eder, *Inflation and Development in Latin America: A Case History of Inflation and Stabilization in Bolivia* (Ann Arbor: University of Michigan, 1968).

31. The exchange rate later moved to 11,880 bolivianos; the currency was renamed peso, with the rate US$1 = 11.88 pesos. This rate was maintained until October 1972.

32. With the elimination of the subsidies, the government froze the prices of four basic items—meat, bread, sugar, and rice—in December 1956. The prices of these items remain unchanged to this day. Needless to say, many of the pulperia goods are sold to black marketeers who "swarm around the company stores like flies around a stable." For a detailed discussion of COMIBOL's pulperias, see Chapter 5.

33. See Eder, *Inflation and Development in Latin America.*

34. Every large mine has hundreds of marginal workers not included in COMIBOL's labor force, who sort and resort rock to remove carefully every bit of mineral. There are also *jucos* (a Quechua word for nocturnal birds of prey) or mineral thieves who sell back to enterprises the mineral ore stolen from them. *Juqueo* (or mineral robbery) has long been practiced in the Bolivian mining industry but especially during the early 1960s. Ore purchased by COMIBOL from these "other sources" increased from 45 tons of tin concentrates in 1957 to 538 tons in 1962 and 1,366 tons in 1964. For details, see Norman Gall, "Bolivia: The Price of Tin. Part II: The Crisis of Nationalization," The American Universities Field Staff Report, vol. 21, no. 2, 1974.

35. See Armando de Urioste, "Asistencia a la Corporación Minera de Bolivia: Un Análisis Crítico de Esfuerzos Pasados y Presentes," report prepared for the World Bank, March 1981.

36. Details on tin smelting in Bolivia are provided in Chapter 6.

37. The implicit tax rate is calculated as $T = 40\ (F - R)/F$, where F is the free market rate and R the official rate.

38. For an analysis of the international competitiveness of Bolivian tin mining in relation to other producers, see Chapter 4.

39. Small mining companies pay less taxes since their "presumed costs" are higher.

40. For a sociological study of the Bolivian mines, see June Nash, *We Eat the Mines and the Mines Eat Us: Dependency and Exploitation in Bolivian Tin Mines* (New York: Columbia University Press, 1979).

CHAPTER 3

The Effect of Tin Mining on the Bolivian Economy

Writing in 1928, Marsh noted, "that humble but indispensable metal (tin) is the hub around which Bolivia's economic life revolves."[1] Fifty-five years later, despite some diversification of the Bolivian economy into hydrocarbons and agriculture, the statement is almost as true. Though the percentage has gone down considerably since the commencement of natural gas exports to Argentina in 1972, tin exports account for more than 35 percent of total merchandise exports (see Table 9). Revenues from tin mining account for 14-15 percent of the total central government tax revenues. In terms of value added, the tin subsector accounts for about 4 percent of gross domestic product (GDP). It has a relatively small share of the total employed labor force (less than 3 percent) but traditionally the mining sector has been in the forefront of the labor movement, in terms of both wage negotiations and sociopolitical concerns.

The purpose of this chapter is to identify and to quantify the contribution of tin mining to the Bolivian economy. More specifically, an attempt is made to examine the influence on Bolivia's domestic aggregate demand of changes in the output and prices of tin, to study the effect of tin revenues on the Treasury's revenues, and to discuss the sector's influence on the rate of inflation and the level of wages in the overall economy. Some discussion of backward and forward linkages is also included. Some of these topics were examined by Gillis and others in their study that used 1973–74 data.[2] Structural and informational developments have occurred since then, however, which warrant an updating of some of their conclusions. In particular, the level and composition of energy costs have changed, there is a somewhat greater use of domestic inputs, and more detailed information has become available on the structure of mining labor's expenditures.

Table 9. *Share of Tin in the Bolivian Economy*

Sector	1970	1975	1980
Tin sector			
Value added as percentage of GDP	5.1	3.8	4.4
Exports as percentage of merchandise exports	44.6	33.6	40.1
Tax revenues as percentage of central government tax revenues	41.2[a]	14.0	15.4
Employment as percentage of total employment	2.8	2.9	2.8
Total mining sector [b]			
Value added as percentage of GDP	9.4	6.7	7.2
Exports as percentage of merchandise exports	89.6	58.6	61.9
Tax revenues as percentage of central government tax revenues	68.1[a]	21.5	24.4
Employment as percentage of total employment	5.2	4.9	4.9

a. Statistical problem relating to payments due from 1969.
b. Including metallurgy.
Sources: Central Bank of Bolivia; Ministry of Finance.

A change in the level of domestic aggregate demand as a result of a change in tin-mining revenues can result from either a change in output or a change in the international price of tin. In the former, a change in the quantity of tin produced will normally result in corresponding changes in the quantity of labor employed and in purchases of energy and material inputs, which, in turn, will lead to further changes in income flows to mine owners (government or private) and tax revenues to the government. By contrast, a change in the price of tin will first affect the income accruing to the mine owners and the government's tax revenues. Should this change in price persist for a reasonably long period, it might also stimulate other changes in the same direction—changes in output as well as in the real wages received by miners and in new investment expenditures.

To estimate the influence on Bolivia's domestic aggregate demand of these two distinct effects, and to analyze the cost structure of the Bolivian economy, a survey was carried out for thirteen medium-size mining firms and thirteen enterprises of COMIBOL that are either sole producers of tin or produce tin along with other minerals. Thus the sample covered at least 90 percent of the total production of tin in Bolivia. For firms that produce other minerals besides tin, input costs attributable to tin production were carefully prorated. A list of the firms included from both the medium-size mining sector and from COMIBOL is provided in Appendix A, and important aggregated results of the survey for the medium-size mines and COMIBOL are presented in Appendix B. Efforts to ensure the reliability of the survey data have already been mentioned in Chapter 1.

The two years chosen for the survey, 1980 and 1981, are the latest for which complete and reliable information could be obtained. The data for 1982 are unreliable because of unresolved accounting problems related to the floating exchange rate, and the subsequent devaluation of the Bolivian peso from US$1 = 25 pesos in early 1982 to US$1 = 200, the rate at which it was fixed in November of that year.

From the available survey data, the weight of each of the costs was obtained, and the import content of each of them estimated. Those cost items for which import intensity was not available from the survey data, were calculated separately on the basis of other available data, and, wherever necessary, further information was gathered from interviews with enterprise managers.

When Gillis and others did their study, no reliable data existed on consumption patterns of Bolivian mine workers. Since then significant work has been done in this area in the context of calculation of the minimum wage. In Table 10, information on the import content of miners' income is provided. The data refer to a family of five. On this basis, the import content of mining labor is 26.1 percent.[3]

The import content of material costs was available from the survey data. Although most of Bolivia's mining inputs are imported, in recent years there has been some increase in the use of domestic inputs, although mine managers frequently complain of the poor quality and relatively high price of domestic inputs compared with imported ones. Some of the main inputs being produced in significant quantity domestically are explosive fuses, steel grinding balls, some foundry goods, electric cables, compressors and drilling equipment, rubber boots, work clothes, and gloves.

Table 10. *Import Content of Bolivian Mine Workers' Consumption*
(Bolivian pesos)

Item	Total expenditure	Import component	Import content of expenditure (percent)
Food	7,635.04	2,240.14	29.3
Clothing	3,748.67	1,237.06	33.0
Education costs	3,370.00	337.00	10.0
Other costs	75.00	50.00	67.0
Total	14,828.71	3,864.20	26.1

Source: Derived from "Estudio Sobre el Salario Mínimo Vital y Escala Móvil Para Trabajadores de la COMIBOL," prepared by CONALSA (Bolivia: La Paz, July 1982.)

Energy costs in Bolivian mining comprise electricity (self-generated as well as purchased) and petroleum costs. In the former, hydroelectric power is the primary source of generation. On the basis of information provided by the National Electricity Company (ENDE), about 80 percent of total annual costs in a hydro-powered electrical system are capital related. Of this, about 90 percent are import costs. The import content of electric energy is, therefore, set at 72 percent.

Bolivia is self-sufficient in petroleum products and has had a small surplus for export, although this surplus has declined gradually since 1974 as production has declined and consumption has increased steadily. In addition, domestic prices of petroleum products are heavily subsidized in Bolivia. For example, the domestic price per barrel of crude oil in 1980 and 1981 was about US$18 and US$26, respectively, at a time when the corresponding export price (f.o.b. Bolivia) in those two years was, respectively, US$29 and US$34 a barrel. Examination of the effect of an increase in purchases of petroleum products on domestic aggregate demand, therefore, requires consideration of (1) the gross increase in aggregate demand because of the use of local petroleum products and (2) the loss to the Bolivian economy because of the subsidized price the tin mining sector pays for petroleum compared with what the country could earn by exporting this product. The change in domestic consumption of petroleum products (dE_p) in the tin mining sector because of a change in gross tin revenues (dS) is therefore provided by

$$dE_p = A_p dS - A_p \left(\frac{P_w - P_d}{P_w} \right) dS$$

$$= A_p \left[1 - \left(\frac{P_w - P_d}{P_w} \right) \right] dS$$

where A_p is the ratio of petroleum costs to gross tin revenues and P_w and P_d are, respectively, the domestic and export price of petroleum. Gillis and others misspecified this part of their model, which may have affected their results.

About 60 percent of smelting costs pertain to energy, divided almost equally among fuel oil, charcoal, and electricity. Other inputs include sodium carbonate, sodium hydroxide, and electrodes, most of which are imported. For smelting and transport costs together, an import intensity of 0.65 was calculated.

"Other costs" is a catchall for several input costs, the more important ones being foreign travel, legal fees, information services, infrastructure, and administration costs. On the basis of separate estimates, the import content of these costs is approximately 44 percent for COMIBOL and 50 percent for medium-size mines. The import content of the other components (profits, interest, and rentals and depreciation expenses) have been similarly derived from interviews with managers, or separate studies, or both.

Finally, to derive the propensity for government to import using tax revenues, a comparison of the foreign exchange purchases (inclusive of foreign debt service payments) was made, which is summarized in Table 11. As the table shows, the import content of central government expenditure has increased steadily, reflecting the proportionally larger payments for external interest and amortization.

Table 12 gives estimates for the various parameters for the two survey years—for COMIBOL and the medium-size mines as well as for the whole sector.

On the basis of this data, it is possible to calculate the initial effect of a change in tin production and sales on the domestic demand for goods and services in Bolivia, using the equation

$$dC_i = (1 - m_i) A_i (1 - A_f) dS,$$

Table 11. *Import Content of Central Government Expenditure*
(US$ millions)

Expenditure	1977	1978	1979	1980	1981
Central government expenditures	400.0	472.0	609.0	765.0	828.0
Central government foreign exchange purchases	45.0	63.0	80.4	115.2	194.3
Import content of central government expenditures (percent)	11.2	13.3	13.2	15.0	23.5

Sources: Central Bank of Bolivia; Ministry of Finance.

where dC_i represents the change in the use of input i as a result of a change in gross tin sales, dS; m_i represents the import intensity of cost i, A_i its proportion in total sales, and A_f the proportion of foreign smelting, transport, and insurance costs in total tin sales. The calculation for petroleum costs is slightly different, and the relevant equation has already been provided. If these equations and data are used, it is estimated that approximately 53 percent of gross tin revenues from increased tin production were spent on domestic goods and services in 1980 and 1981. Put differently, the initial foreign exchange leakages from a change in tin sales because of a change in tin production were approximately 47 percent.

Table 12. *Values of Parameters for Estimating the Effect of Change in Tin Production and Sales on Domestic Aggregate Expenditures, 1980–81*

Parameter description	1980 Medium-size mines	1980 COMIBOL	1980 Total sector	1981 Medium-size mines	1981 COMIBOL	1981 Total sector
As proportion of gross tin sales						
Total labor costs	0.172	0.244	0.228	0.210	0.351	0.319
Material purchases	0.068	0.086	0.082	0.094	0.118	0.112
Total energy costs of which	0.028	0.029	0.029	0.055	0.059	0.058
Electricity[a]	(0.021)	(0.019)	(0.020)	(0.035)	(0.044)	(0.042)
Petroleum products	(0.007)	(0.010)	(0.009)	(0.020)	(0.015)	(0.016)
Domestic smelting and transport costs	0.170	0.166	0.168	0.200	0.228	0.223
Other costs	0.121	0.032	0.057	0.110	0.057	0.069
Profits, financial and rental payments	0.107	0.150	0.134	0.035	-0.012	-0.001
Depreciation expenses	0.050	0.020	0.027	0.047	0.026	0.031
Total tax payments	0.254	0.243	0.245	0.215	0.156	0.169
Foreign smelting, transport and insurance costs	0.030	0.030	0.030	0.034	0.017	0.020
Gross tin sales	1.000	1.000	1.000	1.000	1.000	1.000
Import content of						
Total labor costs	0.261	0.261	0.261	0.261	0.261	0.261
Material purchases	0.770	0.793	0.788	0.763	0.798	0.792
Electricity	0.720	0.720	0.720	0.720	0.720	0.720
Domestic smelting and transport costs	0.650	0.650	0.650	0.650	0.650	0.650
Other costs	0.500	0.450	0.460	0.500	0.450	0.460
Profits, financial and rental payments	0.750	0.700	0.710	0.750	0.700	0.710
Depreciation expenses	0.650	0.400	0.462	0.650	0.400	0.462
Central government expenditures	0.015	0.015	0.015	0.235	0.235	0.235
Price parameters						
Domestic price of crude oil (U.S. dollars a barrel)	18.00	18.00	18.00	26.00	26.00	26.00
World price of crude oil (f.o.b. Bolivia, U.S. dollars a barrel)	29.00	29.00	29.00	34.00	34.00	34.00

a. Purchased as well as self-generated.

The same data can be used to estimate the effect on Bolivian aggregate demand of a change in tin sales arising from a change in international tin prices. Normally, an increase in tin prices will result in an increase in the revenues to the owner of the mines and to the government in the form of additional tax revenues. Under the Bolivian system of compensation, mining labor also shares in any increase in income arising from higher prices. Other costs of mining operations are not normally affected by changes in tin prices.

Under Bolivian mining taxation, approximately 50 percent of any increase in income from a price increase accrues as government revenue. The remaining 50 percent is allocated between wage increases and profits. Mining labor in Bolivia obtains the same share of any increase in income on account of price increases as they do for increases in income arising from increased output. As shown in Table 12, this share for the total sector was 22.8 percent in 1980 and 31.9 percent in 1981. Therefore, the residual of the additional income accruing to the owners of the mines in the form of profits generated by a price increase was 27.2 percent and 18.1 percent in 1980 and 1981, respectively. All other values, except that for the share of foreign smelting, transport, and insurance costs (which is left as in Table 12), are set equal to zero. Substituting these values, the change in domestic expenditures is equal to 65 percent of the change in tin sales in 1980 and 70 percent in 1981, which implies smaller foreign exchange leakages of 35 percent and 30 percent during 1980 and 1981, respectively, compared with the change in domestic expenditures resulting from a change in output. The main reason revenues increase by a greater amount than the proportional increase in prices is the slight progressivity with respect to price of the major mineral tax when prices are not exceptionally high or low.

The analysis of foreign expenditure leakages is concerned only with initial effects. A full general equilibrium analysis of the effect on aggregate demand would require the estimation of a multisectoral econometric model for which data are not available.

Fiscal Result of Tin Revenues

As already mentioned, tax revenues from tin production and export are an important part of the revenues of the Bolivian central government. In addition to the regalias and export taxes, a significant portion of the import duties can be attributed to tin mining. Thus a decline in tin production or price (or both) can have a profound effect on the size of the government deficit. As noted by Gillis and others, this observation—that a decline in an important export product may generate inflationary pressures—is contrary to the prediction of most traditional macroeconomic models.

The inflationary effect of a decline in tin revenues through its impact on the fiscal deficit is clearly moderated by the availability of external financial resources. During 1974–78 international tin prices were rather low, but Bolivia had ready access to foreign commercial loans, so that annual inflation over the period averaged less than 10 percent. By contrast, tin prices rose significantly during 1979–80, but foreign lending declined considerably in view of the country's rapid loss of creditworthiness. Inflation in these two years averaged more than 30 percent a year. As illustrated, when low mineral prices coincide with severe foreign borrowing constraints, a time of crisis ensues, such as the hyperinflationary periods of 1953–57 and 1981–83, when three-digit inflation rates were registered.

Macroeconomic Linkages of Tin Mining

There is little doubt that tin mining in Bolivia has some backward linkages. The development of railways in the first decade of this century and the development of electric energy are the most important examples. But as already noted, about 80 percent of materials needed in tin mining in Bolivia are imported.

In terms of forward linkages, the experience of Bolivia has been mixed. Since the setting up of the National Smelting Company (ENAF), there has been some saving on transport costs and some increase in domestic value added. From the beginning, however, ENAF has been confronted with severe financial and technical problems (see Chapter 6 for details). There has, therefore, been a tradeoff between increasing domestic value added and the inefficiency of domestic smelting. Mineral producers in both the private and public sectors are unanimous in their preference to sell their concentrates directly abroad rather than to ENAF as they are obliged to do by law.

Normally, a mineral-based economy exhibits a marked form of wage dualism, in which the enclave employees in the mineral-exporting sector earn substantially higher wages than those in other sectors of the economy.[4] Nankani has noted that Bolivia has been spared this wage dualism. This is true, however, only if one looks at nominal wages (that is, exclusive of social and other benefits). But, in the nationalized sector of Bolivian mining (which accounts for three-quarters of all mining), a widespread system of subsidized commissaries (*pulperias*) and other social benefits exists (which are discussed in Chapter 5). The prices of four basic food items sold in the mines— bread, rice, meat and sugar—have been frozen since 1956. As an example, in mid-1983 the subsidized price of meat on the rations sold to the miners was three pesos a kilo while the market price of the same item was more than 300 pesos a kilo. It is safe to say that nonwage benefits in 1983 in the nationalized mining sector were at least twice as much as direct wage payments. If these nonwage benefits, which are not available to workers in other sectors of the economy, are added to miners' wages, a significant differential exists between the total earnings of miners and their counterparts in other sectors.

Notes

1. Margaret A. Marsh, *The Bankers in Bolivia: A Study in American Foreign Investment* (New York: AMS Press, 1970).

2. See Malcolm Gillis and others: *Taxation and Mining: Non-fuel Minerals in Bolivia and Other Countries* (Cambridge, Mass.: Ballinger Publishing Company, 1978).

3. Allowance has been made for subsidies on basic food items. It is assumed (realistically) that the savings of mine workers are negligible, at least for the two sample years.

4. For a discussion of this topic and other characteristics of mineral-exporting countries, see Gobind Nankani, *Development Problems of Mineral-Exporting Countries*, World Bank Staff Working Paper no. 354, (Washington, D.C., 1979).

CHAPTER 4

Factors Determining Tin Prices and Competitiveness

In this chapter the principal determinants of international tin prices and the competitiveness of various mining processes and producers are analyzed. A basic framework for determining the price of tin is used—price-cost movements and their relation to the demand for tin. The analysis employs data for the period since the early 1970s.

As with prices of other commodities, the price of tin is determined by a set of factors such as demand functions, production costs, investment policies, and market structure. In the simplest case of price determination in perfectly competitive markets, price is determined at the intersection (A) of the demand curve, DD, and the marginal production cost curves, MM (see Figure 1). This case is presented first. But in the "real world," tin prices are also affected by policy and institutional factors, also discussed in this chapter.

The Demand Curve

Demand for tin is generally a derived one, based on price and income elasticities for its final products. In the production of tinplate, the use of tin can be reduced by material-conserving substitution or can be replaced at the canning stage by competitive materials such as aluminum, tin-free steel (TFS), and plastics.

A recent World Bank study estimated the own-price elasticity and the cross-price elasticity for tinplate at the canning stage as -0.3 and 0.07, respectively.[1] The same study estimated price elasticity at the tinplate production stage (that is, the price elasticity of unit consumption of tin metal for tinplate production) at -0.5. Substitution at the latter stage requires about five years of completion in view of the replacement of old tinning facilities. With both elasticities combined, the long-term price elasticity of tin with respect to its demand for tinplate production is estimated at about -0.9. The elasticity of tin price with respect to its demand in production of solder is much lower than in production of tinplate, because substitution of other materials for tin is more limited in solder production. The overall short-term price elasticity of demand for tin is considered to be in the range of -0.1 to -0.3, and the long-term price elasticity in the range of -0.7 to -1.2, depending upon the ease of substitution and practices of tin uses in tin-consuming industries in various regions. The income elasticity of demand for tin is estimated to be in the range of 0.3 to 0.5.

The important point emerging from these estimates, and which has implications for long-term market prospects for tin, is that, while tin has a low *short-term* price elasticity, it has a relatively high *long-term* price elasticity. In other words, a continually high price for tin in relation to its main substitutes can result in substantial substitution.

The Marginal Production Cost Curve

Before the factors affecting tin production costs are examined, two remarks deserve mention. First, because of difficulties in collecting marginal cost data, average production costs by mining

Figure 1. *Determination of the Price of Tin*

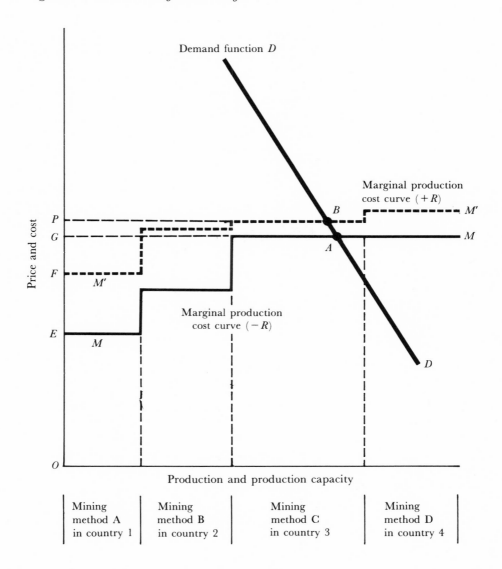

methods are generally employed as a proxy. In this section, average production costs of five mining methods and seven tin-producing countries are used.[2] Second, the established convention in the International Tin Council (ITC) statistics is to express production costs in two forms: production costs, excluding royalties and export duties ($-R$) and production costs, including royalties, export duties, and tributes ($+R$). The same convention is used here.

Production costs ($-R$) are influenced mainly by mining methods, which are determined by mining conditions (metal content of ore, thickness of overburden, and so on) and location. The four principal mining methods are underground mining, dredging, gravel-pump mining, and open-cast mining. Underground mining to extract tin from deep lodes is the most common method of tin mining in Bolivia, the United Kingdom, and Australia. Dredging, the method of mining alluvial deposits, uses floating excavators with a chain of buckets or suction pumps. Dredging can be both onshore and offshore. Gravel-pump mining is a form of open-cast mining, although it is considered different from other types of open-cast mining. In the typical open-cast mine, the ore is mined and the overburden is removed by earth-moving equipment. By contrast, the gravel-pump method,

Table 13. *Production Share and Average Production Costs by Mining Method, 1971-81*

	1971			1974			1978			1981		
	Production share	Production cost (US$/kg)		Production share	Production cost (US$/kg)		Production share	Production cost (US$/kg)		Production share	Production cost (US$/kg)	
Mining method	(percent)	+R	-R	(percent)	+R	-R	(percent)	+R	-R	(percent)	+R	-R
Underground	28.0	3.47	3.21	31.1	6.32	5.00	29.3	11.27	8.94	30.4	14.86	13.26
Gravel pump	38.3	2.43	2.40	36.9	5.35	4.82	39.2	9.37	7.84	42.3	12.01	11.81
Open-cast	15.7	2.91	2.22	2.1	4.79	3.02	2.0	7.97	4.38	2.0	10.21	8.33
Dredges onshore	6.5	2.84	2.33	20.9	4.98	3.41	19.9	8.06	4.89	14.0	9.91	7.56
Dredges offshore	11.6	2.14	1.55	9.1	4.13	3.24	9.6	6.42	4.50	11.3	8.39	6.31
Weighted average	n.a.	3.01	2.48	n.a.	5.86	4.35	n.a.	9.99	7.14	n.a.	13.10	10.89

n.a. Not applicable.

Sources: International Tin Council; and the industry.

commonly used in mining alluvial deposits of Southeast Asia, Nigeria, and Zaire, is relatively labor-intensive and its initial capital requirement is small compared with other open-cast methods. Apart from these four main methods, the traditional method of *dulang* washing is still employed in parts of Southeast Asia and suction boats have recently been developed in southern Thailand. Dulang washing is a traditional method of washing gravel in a bowl (or dulang) for recovering tin. Suction boats are fitted with pipes through which loose sand and gravel are sucked in from the seabed. After tin has been recovered, the waste is discharged over the deck of the boats.

Among the four main methods, gravel pumping accounts for about 40 percent of total tin production; most of the remainder is equally divided between underground mining and dredging.[3] Open-cast mining, once important, has become insignificant recently.

Table 13 provides the average production costs by mining methods for the four benchmark years, 1971, 1974, 1978, and 1981. For the average production costs, which exclude royalties and export duties ($-R$), underground mining has been the highest-cost operation, and offshore dredging the least-cost method.[4] These, however, are *average* figures, and substantial variations can exist within each method.

Among the various countries, average production costs in Bolivia and the United Kingdom have usually been the highest, while those in Thailand and Malaysia have been the lowest (see Table 14).

On the basis of the information available for the four benchmark years, it is possible to construct quasi-marginal production cost curves for each of the four years by plotting the production quantity of each method in each country on the horizontal axis and the average production cost on the vertical axis. These curves are shown in Figures 2 through 5.

To summarize, the highest-cost tin producer is Bolivia, which employs mostly underground mining (the highest-cost method). The lowest-cost producers are Malaysia and Thailand. In Malaysia the majority of tin is produced from on-shore alluvial deposits, for which mining costs are typically lower. Even though off-shore mining is much more significant in Thailand, the mining operations are carried out with large-scale, modern dredges. Moreover, the use of suction boats also reduces average costs.

Policy Factors

In a dynamic framework, a country's cost competitiveness is clearly affected by investments for capacity expansion and modernization. In the present study only the static dimension is considered in which a country can affect its cost-competitiveness only by adjusting taxes and exchange rates.

Competitiveness in international markets depends not just on production costs ($-R$) but on production costs including taxes in a broader sense, that is, royalties, export duties, and tributes ($+R$). Countries can and do affect their competitiveness by adjustments in taxes and duties, as shown in Figure 1. In this figure, $M'M'$ denotes the production cost, including taxes and duties ($+R$) for each country and mining method. With taxes, the price is determined at the level P, that is, at the intersection of the production cost ($+R$) of the marginal producer and the given demand curve. In such a case, the economic rent accruing to Country 1 by Method A, for example, is shown as the distance between E and P. This rent can be further itemized into (1) GP, which corresponds to long-term scarcity of tin resources (scarcity rent) and to collusive action by producers (monopoly rent); and (2) EG, which corresponds to the so-called differential rent accruing to efficient producers. The more efficient the producer, the greater is the differential rent. Also, in the case of Country 1 and Method A, a tax EP can be levied without jeopardizing its cost-competitiveness by that method.

On the basis of historical data used to construct Figures 2 through 5, two observations can be made. First, no economic rent accrued to the marginal producers in 1971 and 1981, whereas significant rents accrued to them in 1974 and 1978. Second, export duties in those countries which have such duties (all except the United Kingdom, Australia, and Zaire) remained fixed in absolute terms, regardless of increases in production costs. Consequently, the percentage of export duties in

Table 14. *Production Share and Average Production Costs by Country, 1971–81*

	1971			1974			1978			1981		
	Production share	Production cost (US$/kg)		Production share	Production cost (US$/kg)		Production share	Production cost (US$/kg)		Production share	Production cost (US$/kg)	
Country	(percent)	+R	−R	(percent)	+R	−R	(percent)	+R	−R	(percent)	+R	−R
Bolivia	19.4	3.80	3.47	22.7	6.71	5.03	22.8	12.53	9.54	20.2	16.69	14.44
United Kingdom	1.2	3.84	3.75	2.3	5.57	5.50	2.0	8.75	8.39	3.0	13.24	12.70
Indonesia	8.7	3.17	2.87	13.3	5.82	5.03	18.3	9.33	8.11	20.8	12.67	10.43
Thailand	18.3	2.38	1.67	11.3	5.09	3.44	10.5	8.82	5.09	10.8	12.39	9.08
Malaysia	46.0	2.94	2.26	45.5	5.74	3.91	41.1	9.71	5.96	37.1	12.09	9.69
Australia	6.5	2.56	2.56	4.9	5.13	5.11	5.5	6.44	6.24	7.9	10.81	10.51
Zaire	..	..	..	..	..	..	..	..	..	0.3	9.51	9.51
Weighted average	n.a.	3.01	2.48	n.a.	5.86	4.35	n.a.	9.99	7.14	n.a.	13.10	10.89

n.a. Not applicable.
.. Not available.

Sources: International Tin Council; and the industry.

Figure 2. *Average Production Costs (+R) and (−R) by Mining Method, by Country, and by Price of Tin, 1971*

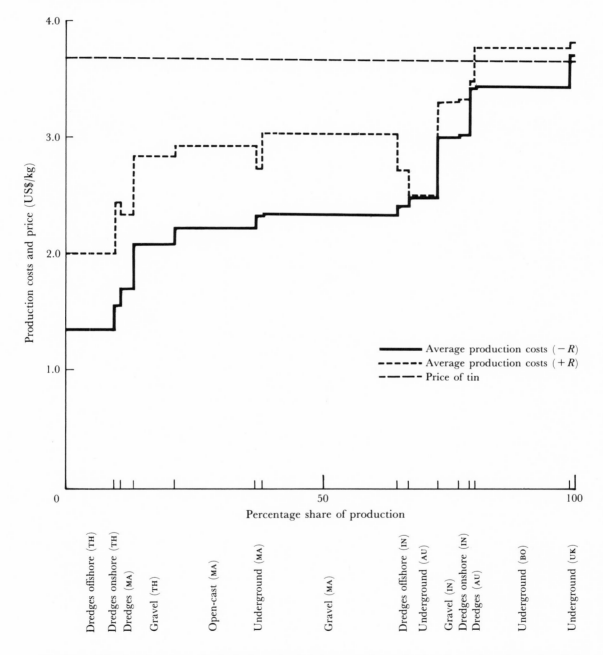

Note: The width of each category in the horizontal axis is in proportion to its share in total producton by all the categories listed here. Country names are abbreviated: AU is Australia; BO, Bolivia; IN, Indonesia; MA, Malaysia; TH, Thailand; UK, United Kingdom.

Source: World Bank data.

Figure 3. *Average Production Costs ($-R$) and ($+R$) by Mining Method, by Country, and by Price of Tin, 1974*

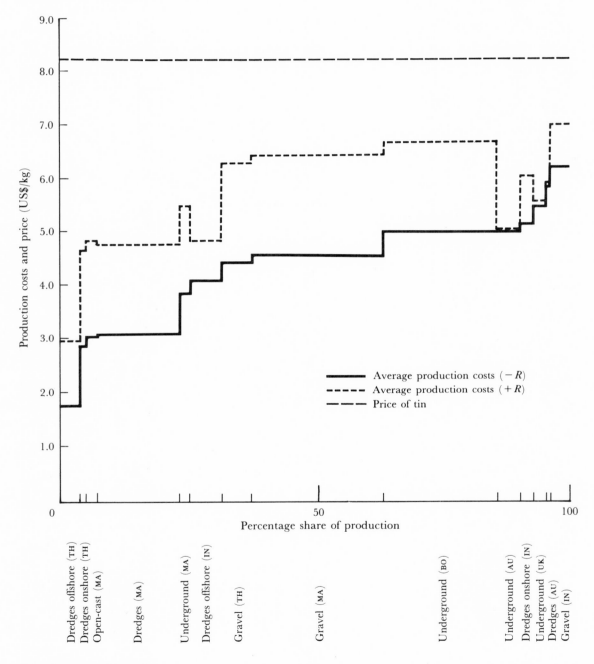

Note: See note to Figure 2.
Source: World Bank data.

Figure 4. *Average Production Costs (−R) and (+R) by Mining Method, by Country, and by Price of Tin, 1978*

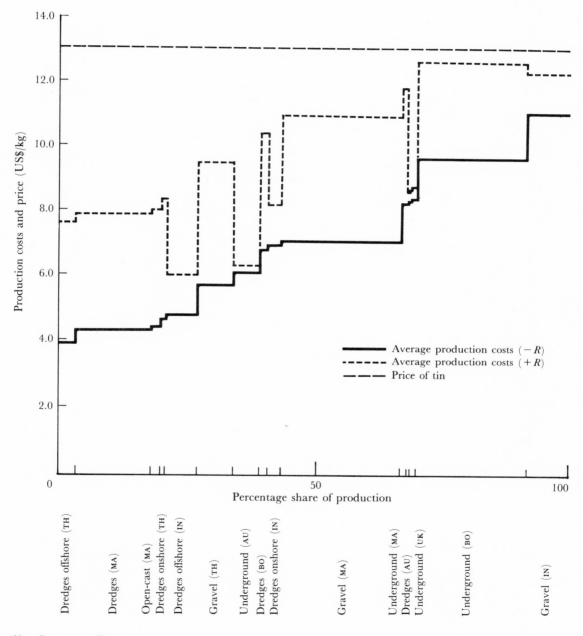

Note: See note to Figure 2.
Source: World Bank data.

Figure 5. *Average Production Costs (−R) and (+R) by Mining Method, by Country, and by Price of Tin, 1981*

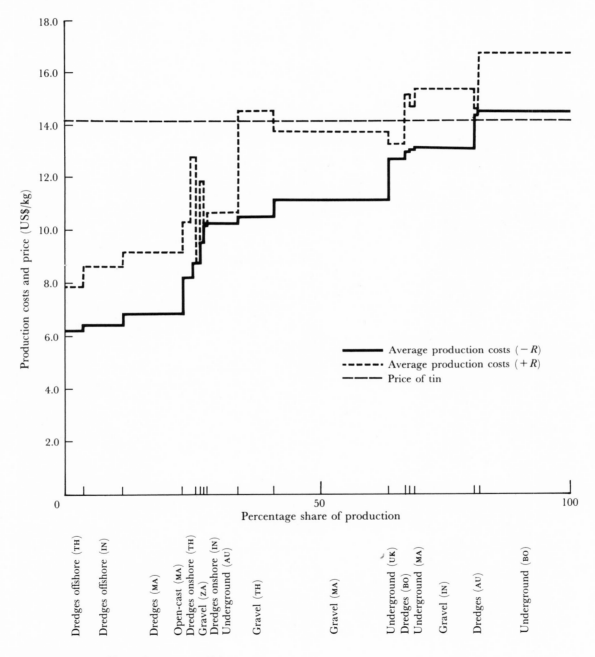

Note: See note to Figure 2. ZA means Zaire.
Source: World Bank data.

total production costs $(+R)$ was generally higher for low-cost producers (between 20 percent and 30 percent) than for high-cost producers (about 10 percent).

Exchange rate policy is the second policy variable that affects export competitiveness. The degree of over- and undervaluation of a country's currency can significantly affect its competitiveness.[5] For example, between 1978 and 1981 the exchange rate adjustments of the Bolivian currency lagged behind the inflation rate, while the exchange rates of the other tin-producing countries were revised more significantly than their inflation rates. Table 15 summarizes the adjusted costs that represent the "true" competitiveness, after the different degrees of over- or undervaluation of the various countries are taken into account. As can be seen from the table, with this adjustment, Bolivia—the highest-cost producer—slips into the middle-cost range, whereas Malaysia and Australia become somewhat higher-cost producers.

Institutional Factors

Two institutional factors have an important effect on the international price of tin: the operations of the ITC and the General Services Administration (GSA) sales of the U.S. strategic stockpile of tin.

Tin is unique among metals in the sense that its producers and consumers have an international commodity agreement. The ITC has so far employed two means to stabilize the price of tin. In the first, the price band with buffer stock operations, the ITC attempts to restrict movement of the price of tin within the ranges specified by the ITC. The second method is that of export controls, under which each producing country's export quota is generally determined by multiplying the export tonnage of the country in the preceding periods by a predetermined ratio. Although the buffer stock operations and export controls are intended to stabilize prices and they are decided by both producing and consuming countries, there is no a priori guarantee that the intended price would be an equilibrium price, that is, that it would coincide with the intersection of the demand curve

Table 15. *Actual and Adjusted Tin Production Cost $(-R)$, 1981*
(US$/Kg)

Country and mining method[a]		Actual production cost $(-R)$	Adjustment factor[b]	Adjusted production cost $(-R)$
(BO)	Underground	14.5	0.73	10.6
(AU)	Dredges	14.4	1.05	15.2
(IN)	Gravel pump	13.1	1.22	16.1
(MA)	Underground	13.0	1.14	14.9
(BO)	Dredges	13.0	0.73	9.5
(UK)	Underground	12.7	0.88	11.2
(MA)	Gravel pump	11.2	1.14	12.8
(TH)	Gravel pump	10.5	1.01	10.6
(AU)	Lode underground	10.3	1.05	10.8
(ZA)	Open cast	10.2	1.82	18.5
(IN)	Dredges offshore	9.6	1.22	11.8
(ZA)	Gravel pump	8.9	1.82	16.2
(TH)	Dredges onshore	8.7	1.01	8.7
(MA)	Open cast	8.2	1.14	9.4
(MA)	Dredge	6.8	1.14	7.8
(IN)	Dredges onshore	6.4	1.22	7.8
(TH)	Dredges offshore	6.2	1.82	11.3

a. See note to Figure 2 for meaning of country abbreviations.
b. The inverse of the degree of "overvaluation" between 1978 and 1981.
Sources: Computed on the basis of data from the International Tin Council; unpublished data from the tin industry; and the International Monetary Fund, *International Financial Statistics* (Washington, D.C., various issues).

and the marginal production cost curve. Controversy over whether the ITC's price stabilization efforts have, in fact, supported the price of tin has arisen from time to time.

The effect of buffer stock operations and export controls varies from country to country. Figure 6 illustrates the consequences of buffer stock operations. If the preoperation price, $\overline{P}$, is lower than the floor price, P_f, the price is forced to rise to the floor price level, the quantity $Q_f\overline{Q}$ being withdrawn from the market. With increased stocks, marginal producers will face strong pressures to cut their production. By contrast, export controls stipulate proportionate decreases in exports (equivalent to production in most cases) of all producers.

Recent buffer stock operations and export controls of the ITC are shown in Table 16. The percentage of net purchases or sales to total production varies between 1 percent and 5 percent in most years. But in 1975 and 1982, two years of depressed markets, the ratio of purchases was about 10 percent and 24 percent, respectively, whereas in 1976, a year of higher prices, the ratio of sales amounted to about 9 percent.

Sales from the U.S. strategic stockpile of tin conducted by the GSA is the other important factor affecting prices. Except for 1965, 1966, 1973, and 1974, when GSA sold large amounts of tin, the

Figure 6. *Tin Price Determination with Buffer Stock Operations*

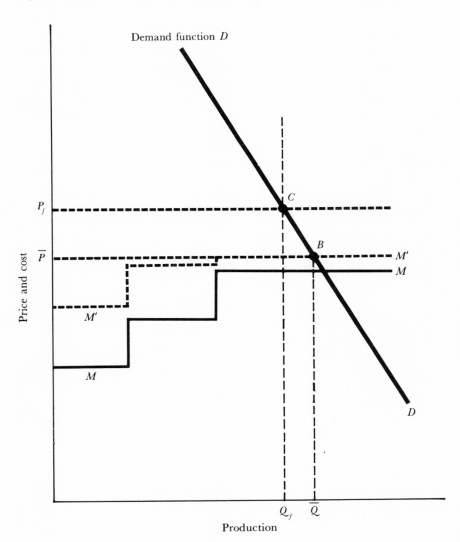

percentage of GSA sales to total supply has ranged between 1 percent and 3 percent (Table 16). Nonetheless, the threat of potential GSA sales depresses prices, and producing countries have frequently complained about GSA sales.

A Review of the World Tin Economy over the Past Decade

Within the preceding framework, it is interesting to analyze the behavior of the world tin economy over the past decade. In the early 1970s both consumption and production of tin were still increasing. By the mid-1970s a moderately declining trend set in. At the same time, production costs, both $(+R)$ and $(-R)$, increased in real terms almost across the board between 1971 and 1978. Significantly, the costs of the high-cost producers increased much faster than those of other producers (see Table 17). But even the high-cost producers were able to pass a larger proportion of the cost increases to consumers. Between 1978 and 1981 production costs continued to increase across the board—but the price did not increase in proportion. For the first time in the period under review, the price in 1981 could not cover all the production costs $(+R)$ of the high-cost producers.

To analyze the cost increase over the period 1971–81, we calculated the percentage shares of the contribution of the cost increase due to internal factors (increases in production costs in real and local currency terms and increases in taxes) and those due to external factors (overvaluation of the local currency and world inflation) for the two highest-cost operations: Bolivian lode underground and Indonesian gravel pump, (see Table 18). In the Bolivian case, the cost increase was equally the result of internal and external factors, whereas in the Indonesian case, only a quarter of the cost increase was due to internal factors.

The relative price of tin with respect to aluminum rose significantly in the latter half of the 1970s, as distinct from the smoothly increasing historical trend. Substitution at the canning stage by aluminum and material-conserving substitution at the tinplate production stage accelerated. As a

Table 16. *ITC Buffer Stock Operations, Export Controls, and GSA Sales, 1965–82*

Year	Buffer stock operations (tons) Net purchases	Net sales	Number of months of effective export controls	GSA sales (tons)
1965	0	0	0	21,733
1966	36	0	0	16,276
1967	4,795	0	0	6,146
1968	6,640	0	4	3,495
1969	0	6,807	12	2,048
1970	0	3,432	0	3,038
1971	5,405	0	0	1,736
1972	5,842	0	0	361
1973	0	11,478	9	19,949
1974	0	859	0	23,137
1975	19,929	0	9	575
1976	0	19,265	6	3,586
1977	0	806	0	2,635
1978	0	0	0	326
1979	0	0	0	0
1980	0	0	0	25
1981	3,865	2,875	0	5,920
1982	53,330	1,663	9	4,172

Source: The International Tin Council, *Tin Statistics* (various issues).

Table 17. *Production Costs (+ R) and (− R) and Prices, 1971–81*
(1980 constant US$/kg)

Production cost and prices	1971	1974	1978	1981
High-cost producers[a]				
+R	11.0	12.0	15.3	17.3
−R	10.0	9.5	12.3	14.9
Average-cost producers[b]				
+R	8.8	10.5	12.1	13.8
−R	7.3	7.8	8.6	11.4
Low-cost producers[a]				
+R	7.2	8.1	8.5	9.3
−R	5.5	5.3	5.3	7.0
Actual price[c]	10.3	14.6	15.6	14.9
ITC floor price	11.8	11.4	13.7	12.6
ITC ceiling price	9.6	9.3	10.9	16.4

a. The weighted average production costs of the 25th percentile measured in (− R).

b. The weighted average of all producers.

c. LME settlement price, standard grade.

Sources: International Tin Council; and unpublished data from the tin industry.

Table 18. *Classification of Cost Increases in the Tin-Mining Industry in Bolivia and Indonesia, 1971–81*
(percent)

	1971–78	1978–81
Bolivia (lode underground)		
Internal factors		
Real cost increases in the tin industry	31.1	− 127.2
Increases in taxes	24.4	− 31.2
Subtotal	55.5	− 158.4
External factors		
Overvaluation of the local currency	10.4	125.3
World inflation	34.1	133.1
Subtotal	44.5	258.4
Total	100.0	100.0
Indonesia (gravel pump)		
Internal factors		
Real cost increases in the tin industry	18.5	7.3
Increases in taxes	7.8	29.3
Subtotal	26.3	36.6
External factors		
Overvaluation of the local currency	36.9	− 20.2
World inflation	36.8	83.6
Subtotal	73.7	63.4
Total	100.0	100.0

Sources: Computed on the basis of data from the International Tin Council; unpublished data from the tin industry; and the International Monetary Fund, *International Financial Statistics* (Washington, D.C., various issues).

Table 19. *Trade Flows of Tin, 1970 and 1981*

(tons)

	Importing country															
Exporting country	United States and Canada		Western Europe		Japan and East Asia[a]		Southeast Asia,[b] China, and Australia		Latin America		CPEs[c]		Others		Total	
	1970	1981	1970	1981	1970	1981	1970	1981	1971	1981	1971	1981	1971	1981	1971	1981
Bolivia	3,561	10,930	23,675	8,611	0	0	0	0	76	399	827	1,638	1,542	1,894	29,681	23,472
Other Latin American countries	396	1,556	0	2,389	0	0	0	0	0	1,521	0	480	0	0	396	5,946
Southeast Asia, China, and Australia	52,283	30,673	36,937	58,777	27,811	33,897	15,776	21,980	1,155	652	5,330	7,722	4,266	8,975	143,558	162,676
Africa	930	520	16,990	4,380	0	0	0	40	0	0	111	0	1,980	809	20,011	5,749
United States and Canada	582	2,626	80	2,761	0	0	0	156	482	676	0	0	3,648	909	4,792	7,134
Western Europe	698	491	12,555	6,471	0	0	0	0	27	261	8,454	5,191	850	817	22,584	13,231
Total	58,450	46,796	90,237	83,389	27,811	33,903	15,776	22,176	1,740	3,509	14,722	15,031	12,286	13,404	221,022	218,208

Note: Tin is tin concentrates and tin metal combined.
a. Includes the Republic of Korea, Hong Kong, and China.
b. Includes Malaysia, Indonesia, Thailand, Singapore, Burma, the Philippines, and Laos.
c. Centrally planned economies.
Source: International Tin Council, *Tin Statistics 1970–80* and *Tin Statistics 1971–81.*

result of both substitution and the start of the economic recession in 1980, consumption began to decline significantly during 1978–81.

Under these circumstances, a squeeze on high-cost producers became visible. Changes were brought about by eliminating the export tax in Bolivia and by adjusting the real exchange rate in Indonesia.

Relative changes in production costs, exchange rates, and other factors among exporting countries and varying rates of growth rates in importing countries can alter the pattern of trade in tin. To analyze the main aspects of these changes in trade patterns during the past decade, trade flow matrices (for tin metal and tin concentrates combined) were constructed for 1970 and 1981 for six exporting and seven importing countries and regions (see Table 19).[6]

Among the major exporting countries and regions, a significant decrease of quantity exported was registered in Bolivia and Africa, whereas Southeast Asian countries, China, and Australia, and other Latin American countries (namely, Brazil) increased their exports considerably. For importing countries and regions, there was a decrease in Western Europe and North America, whereas imports by East Asia (principally Japan, the Republic of Korea, and China) and the centrally planned economies increased.

Despite changes in the quantities of tin traded, however, the overall pattern of tin trade has remained unchanged. Exports from southeast Asia, China and Australia were exported to all regions, whereas Africa exported, almost exclusively, to Western European countries. Bolivia exported to Western Europe and North America, but not to the two fastest growing regions: East Asia and the centrally planned economies. Since average transport costs account for only a small portion of tin prices, the trade-flow pattern is probably the result of historical marketing practices rather than purely economic factors.

Notes

1. Hideo Hashimoto, *Modeling Material Substitution in the Tin-Tinplate-TFS Complex* (Washington, D.C., World Bank Commodity Division, 1983).

2. The seven countries included are Australia, Bolivia, Indonesia, Malaysia, Thailand, the United Kingdom, and Zaire.

3. These data refer only to ITC member countries.

4. Excluding the less important open-cast mining in 1974 and 1978.

5. The degree of overvaluation of the currency of Country A in a given period is computed as the change in consumer prices in Country A in relation to the change in U.S. consumer prices, divided by the change in the exchange rate of Country A in relation to the U.S. dollar.

6. The trade flow matrices for tin concentrates and tin metal for 1965, 1970, 1975, and 1981 are presented in the Statistical Appendix.

CHAPTER 5

Problems of COMIBOL

Since its inception in 1952, COMIBOL has been beset by a series of problems, some emanating from its own internal organization and administrative and financial problems, others the result of impositions on it by the government. Particularly in recent years, COMIBOL's production of various minerals has declined considerably, and, as can be seen from Table 20, it has suffered financial losses even before taxes. In this chapter, an effort is made to find out why, despite the reasonably high technical caliber of COMIBOL staff since its beginnings, the corporation has encountered such serious problems. Some recommendations are also provided for improving performance.[1]

Major Problems of COMIBOL

Unlike some of its foreign counterparts that specialize by mineral, COMIBOL is a multimineral corporation. Its management, therefore, faces highly complex and diverse technical issues, difficult to resolve even for experienced multinational corporations. To deal with these technical issues, while administering a comprehensive social program for its employees and assuming responsibilities for marketing and investment, requires a high level of managerial and commercial efficiency as well

Table 20. *COMIBOL, Overall Deficit of 1978–82*
(US$ millions)

Revenue, costs, and expenditure	1978	1979	1980	1981
Total sales revenue	329.6	420.8	355.4	384.9
Marketing costs	97.1	101.3	83.1	102.0
Transport	14.5	13.1	9.9	16.5
Smelting	53.6	51.0	38.6	57.8
Penalties	29.0	37.2	34.6	27.7
Net sales	232.5	319.5	272.3	282.9
Operating costs	159.0	186.3	233.8	293.5
Labor costs	67.3	81.6	84.2	113.3
Materials	27.5	30.2	31.1	45.8
Utilities	6.2	6.9	7.2	14.6
Depreciation	6.2	7.3	7.9	10.0
Mineral purchases	29.5	35.7	23.4	42.6
Interest payments	14.1	16.0	19.1	27.4
Others	8.2	8.6	60.9	39.8
Current surplus before taxes	73.5	133.2	38.5	− 10.6
Taxes	83.7	105.0	72.5	47.5
Current account deficit	− 10.2	28.2	− 34.0	− 58.1
Capital expenditures	45.6	32.8	5.6	8.0
Overall deficit	− 55.8	− 61.0	− 39.6	− 66.1

Source: COMIBOL.

as an advanced system of cost control. COMIBOL does not possess many of these attributes. The main problems of COMIBOL may be classified as those arising from its organizational and management structure, its manpower and remuneration policies, a suboptimal level of investment, excessive taxation, and a heavy debt burden.[2]

Organizational and Management Problems

Many of COMIBOL's financial problems stem from a heavy reliance on social objectives. Because of political and trade union pressures and the very circumstances of the corporation's birth, COMIBOL's objective of providing employment and services to its labor force has been historically paramount, and many financially unprofitable mines have been kept open (subsidized by the more profitable ones) for purely social reasons. Conditions in the mines make this emphasis understandable. Nor would it necessarily be a problem if COMIBOL could provide the social services at lower social costs than could the responsible government agencies, and if the provision of the services would not interfere unduly with COMIBOL's productive activities. But as shown later, COMIBOL's social objectives and activities considerably affect what should be its principal objective of increasing production. The corporation is essentially responsible for fourteen mining enterprises, some industrial plants for the manufacture of spare parts, a volatilization plant, electricity generating plants, a railroad company (Ferrocorp), and agencies abroad responsible for procurement and negotiations with metal traders. In the management of these diverse activities, COMIBOL suffers simultaneously from excessive centralization in some activities and too little central control in others. For example, the centralization of all activities related to maintenance and procurement, as well as financial and auditing control, implies excessive reliance on the La Paz and Oruro offices and, consequently, an excessive amount of time to complete these activities. As a rule, the technical manager is involved in too many routine decisions, which leave him little time for planning, coordination, and control functions. Under the present system, the manager of an enterprise exercises little control over factors of production, and with authority removed, so is the responsibility and much of the interest of the manager. By contrast, the manufacture of spare parts is excessively dispersed among small industrial units, which lowers efficiency and quality and raises costs. Also, it would make sense to have all sales conducted by a centralized body because of the complexity of this activity and the economies of scale achieved by centralization.

Past decentralization efforts have been geographical, such as the transfer of the Operations Division (Gerencia de Operaciones) and the Auxiliary Engineering Services Unit (Ingenieria Auxiliar) to Oruro.[3] This transfer was not accompanied by actual delegation of responsibility. Thus, although a spare part may be manufactured at Oruro, clearance for orders for these by enterprises must come from La Paz. This creates unnecessary bureaucractic steps and costly delays.

Another related factor is the excessive government interference in the activities of COMIBOL. Every change in government is invariably accompanied by a change of the general manager and his senior staff. Over the period 1978–80, COMIBOL had eight general managers. In each mining enterprise, there are interventores of the Auditor General's Office, who exercise excessive control, with dubious results, on many operations, and affect the morale of enterprise managers. Similarly, bidding and procurement procedures are excessively complicated and time-consuming. Each invitation to tender must have responses from at least three suppliers, and since on many occasions there may not be the required three suppliers, the process of retendering repeatedly can be time-consuming. Moreover, the procurement of even relatively small items involves at least sixty stages before being processed at La Paz. It takes more than a year from the date of acquisition for the materials to reach the enterprise. Consequently, there is a tendency to overorder materials. The total inventory in COMIBOL (in the central warehouse as well as the enterprises) is estimated at more than US$80 million, and many of the items are obsolete.

Other related problems are absence of clear delegation of authority, excessive loss of time in resolving unforeseen problems because of improper planning, little exchange of information because of scarce horizontal contacts and interchange among managers, too many organizational levels, and an excessive number of advisers and assistants.

In mid-1983 the government and the Miners' Federation reached an agreement under which there would be workers' participation in the board of directors of COMIBOL. Under the system, four of the seven directors of the corporation would be named by the federation, giving it the majority of votes (*cogestión mayoritaria*). Although the participation of representatives of the mine workers can be beneficial to production and worker discipline, it can also lead to increased politicization of COMIBOL. It is too early to assess the effect of the change on COMIBOL's performance.

Problems Related to Manpower and Remuneration Policies

For social reasons, some of COMIBOL's mines, especially Catavi, Unificada, and Colquiri, have to support a considerably larger labor force than they actually require. Staff has been increased even in years of falling production. At the same time, the share of the work force employed underground is about 40 percent (see Table 21), compared with about 60 percent in private mining companies. Labor relations traditionally have been strained, and strikes and unannounced work stoppages are frequent. Absenteeism is a problem, though not a serious one when compared with mining companies in other countries. Written rules and procedures do not exist for overtime, and practice varies from mine to mine (although, in general, the practice is to pay double rate for overtime). Apparently there are strong pressures on supervisory staff to grant overtime.

Until recently, COMIBOL had no less than sixteen salary regimes. Apart from this, COMIBOL also has a two-tier profit-sharing plan, one at the mining enterprise level and another at the COMIBOL level. The first bonus is paid monthly to enterprise employees as 25 percent of the enterprise profits and has no limit; the second bonus is paid annually to all COMIBOL employees from the corporation's annual profits and is limited to 100 percent of annual salary. This system is faulty because it may bear no relation to productivity or effort but, rather, reflect price fluctuations. Moreover, payment may be very high in a month prior to which, or after which, profits have been, or will be, low or negative.

Table 21. *Employment in COMIBOL Mines, 1982*

	Employees					Underground as a percentage of total
Mine	Underground	Concentrator	Surface	Education and health	Total	
Catavi	1352	894	1442	779	4467	30.3
Quechisla	1872	612	1398	671	4553	41.1
Colquiri	1000	393	718	346	2457	40.7
Huanuni	982	361	458	316	2117	46.4
Unificada	837	315	564	189	1905	43.9
San Jose	626	306	464	320	1716	36.5
Caracoles	589	123	277	138	1127	52.3
Santa Fe	353	167	251	130	901	39.1
Coroco	465	68	312	108	953	48.8
Viloco	298	101	222	105	726	41.0
Bolivar	258	75	139	58	530	48.7
Colquechaca	167	60	101	32	360	46.4
Matilde	312	47	189	68	616	50.6
Colavi	215	0	118	32	365	58.9
Total	9,326	3,522	6,653	3,292	22,793	40.92

Note: Totals do not include about 3,000 COMIBOL employees who do not work in the mines.
Source: COMIBOL.

In addition, COMIBOL runs a widespread program of social services. For example, there are currently more than 60,000 students in various COMIBOL schools, with a student-teacher ratio of 25:1. The corporation provides school supplies such as pencils, books, blackboards, and maps, as well as free breakfast, subsidized uniforms, and some scholarships. In view of the physical isolation of many of the mines, the provision of education by COMIBOL is not only justifiable but also necessary. But much of the emphasis of the education is on humanities and little on technical and industrial topics, which are more relevant to the students' lives in the mines. This may partly explain the high dropout rate in the schools. Also, there is a general lack of control over educational costs.

COMIBOL also provides housing for its employees, and when there is a shortage, subsidized rentals. With the increase in the cost of construction, the corporation opted for imported prefabricated houses. But when the exchange rate was adjusted, these became unaffordable. Besides, they entail a great deal of effort and money in land preparation and infrastructure and are not generally liked by the miners.

COMIBOL provides the infrastructure both in La Paz and in the mines for specialized medical and dental services. Health and related services currently employ 1,400 persons, of whom about 250 are doctors. Again, the cost control systems are inadequate: the employer and employee contributions cover only one-third of the total medical costs.

An important employee benefit is the provision of subsidized basic needs items through company stores. In 1952 COMIBOL sold thirty-five different commodities at highly subsidized prices. In 1956, however, the prices of four of these items were frozen in nominal (peso) terms. To this day, the prices of these four items—meat, sugar, bread and rice—are frozen at the 1956 levels, with COMIBOL absorbing the commissary loss (*perdida pulperia*). In view of the large increases in their market prices, COMIBOL has to bear an ever increasing deficit. Tables 22 and 23 show the differences between the two sets of prices for 1982 and mid-1983. The system of pulperias varies from mine to mine; in some the quota or ration is fixed on a per capita basis and in others on the basis of household numbers. Prices of the items also vary among the mines because of transport and inventory cost differences. For other essential goods, prices are set at slightly above wholesale prices. Clearly the longer the 1956 prices are maintained and the higher the market prices for these items, the larger are the commissary losses borne by COMIBOL, which amounted to about US$20 million in 1981.

Table 22. *Subsidized Unit Costs of Four Basic Food Items*
(Bolivian pesos)

Mining enterprise	Sugar (kilo)	Rice (kilo)	Meat (kilo)	Bread (about 120 grams)
Catavi	1.17	1.30	2.82	0.11
Quechisla	0.99	1.10	2.43	0.13
Huanuni	0.99	1.10	2.70	0.11
Colquiri	0.99	1.10	3.00	0.13
Unificada	1.58	1.08	2.72	0.20
San Jose	0.99	1.10	2.50	0.14
Caracoles	0.99	1.20	2.70	0.15
Santa Fe	0.99	1.36	3.00	0.15
Viloco	0.90	1.00	2.80	0.11
Corocoro	1.26	1.19	2.49	0.12
Rio Yura	0.99	1.10	2.80	0.13
Adm. Oruro	1.13	1.41	2.50	0.14
Bolivar	0.99	1.36	3.00	0.15
Pulacayo	0.99	1.10	2.80	0.13
Bolsa Negra	1.22	0.99	2.70	0.15

Note: These unit costs have been frozen since December 1956. The difference between these prices and the market price at any point is the per unit commissary loss to COMIBOL.
Source: COMIBOL.

Table 23. *Actual Unit Costs (Market Prices) of Four Basic Items*
(Bolivian pesos)

Mining enterprise	Sugar per kilo		Rice per kilo		Meat per kilo		Bread (about 120 grams)	
	Average 1982	May 1983	Average 1982	May 1983	Average 1982	May 1983	Average 1982	May 1983
Catavi	49.90	69.67	66.95	63.20	139.50	342.94	1.60	6.20
Quechisla	49.99	75.90	65.70	130.00	140.00	310.62	1.66	6.00
Huanuni	41.71	73.59	27.61	74.76	121.36	330.28	1.80	4.35
Colquiri	25.80	76.38	21.19	76.69	120.00	341.01	1.45	7.06
Unificada	26.52	69.53	34.66	97.15	146.76	314.05	1.88	7.12
San Jose	27.00	71.85	34.00	80.00	146.00	323.52	1.80	6.50
Caracoles	50.75	73.45	22.10	75.48	179.23	322.61	1.60	6.50
Santa Fe	54.80	76.50	72.20	76.87	207.75	264.89	1.60	7.09
Viloco	54.79	73.74	72.42	75.87	234.70	320.40	1.60	5.20
Corocoro	35.67	74.65	72.07	88.16	207.74	331.11	1.82	6.00
Rio Yura	52.00	76.25	79.64	103.23	211.11	289.29	3.63	9.67
Adm. Oruro	47.92	77.59	66.35	74.36	117.31	340.00	1.93	8.00
Bolivar	47.80	76.48	70.80	73.87	118.00	341.60	1.90	5.95
Pulacayo	70.96	76.00	92.18	82.23	241.49	319.58	2.50	8.70
Bolsa Negra	44.96	70.83	82.65	86.82	190.00	305.00	2.80	6.00

Source: COMIBOL.

Lack of Investment

Because of COMIBOL's financial problems, the level of investment has been abysmally low, particularly during the past several years: investment averaged about US$5 million a year for the period 1980–82, although gross annual sales averaged about US$330 million over the same period. When the mining industry was nationalized in 1952, much of COMIBOL's equipment was already depreciated and technically obsolete. One cannot but marvel at the genius of COMIBOL's maintenance crews who manage to make "museum pieces" work.

Systematic exploration and mine development has also been neglected. Most deposits being mined today were known at the turn of the century. Except for a short period during the mid-1960s, there has been no significant exploratory activity—partly because of political instability (which particularly affects this high-risk, high-cost activity requiring a relatively long gestation period) and partly because of an unresponsive tax system that provides no incentives for exploration. Compared with mining companies in other countries, COMIBOL's expenditures on exploration (which rarely reached 0.5 percent of gross sales in any particular year) are very low.[4]

As a result, known reserves of most mines have fallen to very low levels. Only in a few mines have reserves been developed for more than three or four years of production. Furthermore, recovery rates of metallic values have declined as lower-grade, more complex ores are being mined. Table 24 summarizes COMIBOL's tin reserves. From the economic point of view, only the reserves classified as "accessible" (proved and probable) can be considered available; the remaining reserves require varying degrees of additional investment for their development.

Excessive Taxation

Excessive taxation is examined in detail in Chapter 7. Suffice it to note here that, until recently, COMIBOL has had profits before taxes in most years, and that in most years the combined burden of the various taxes paid by COMIBOL has exceeded 100 percent of pretax profits.

Table 24. *Summary of COMIBOL's Tin Reserves, End 1982*

Classification	Mineral ore (dry tons)	Percentage tin	Metal (fine tons)
Accessible (proved)	4,304,823	1.23	50,797
Accessible (probable)	6,168,566	1.37	84,509
Inaccessible[a]	3,565,676	1.38	49,206
Subtotal underground	14,039,065	1.31	184,512
Mine tailings (Desmontes)	30,799,238	0.30	92,397
Mill washings (Relaves)	61,950,251	0.43	266,386
Placer deposits (Veneros)	327,574,784	0.01	32,757
Subtotal surface	420,324,273	0.09	391,540
Total reserves	434,363,338	0.13	576,052

a. Includes proved and probable.
Source: COMIBOL.

Heavy Debt Burden

COMIBOL's total debt outstanding and disbursed at the end of 1982 was about US$278 million, including about US$150 million of external debt. This does not include cumulated arrears at the end of 1982 of about US$80 million consisting of nonpayment to the National Power Company (ENDE) for electricity supply, to the National Railways Corporation (ENFE) for transport charges, to the Treasury for nonpayment of taxes, and to others. If these arrears are added to the total, the total debt increases to about US$360 million. Table 25 provides details on this debt. Debt servicing is a heavy financial burden on the corporation: in 1982, for example, COMIBOL paid about US$80 million in interest, commissions, and amortization on its total debt, which amounted to over a quarter of its gross sales in that year.

To summarize, because of various factors, some beyond COMIBOL's control, the corporation has experienced severe financial problems that have affected its long-term development and exploration plans. Unless a concerted effort is made by the corporation and the government to rehabilitate COMIBOL financially and administratively, there is a strong likelihood that the entity will continue to experience declining production and increasing losses, which, in one form or another, will have to be borne by the Bolivian Treasury.

Some Recommendations for Changes in COMIBOL

From its inception, COMIBOL has been saddled with social objectives and functions that are not part of the duties of a commercially run enterprise. This is peculiar neither to COMIBOL nor to Bolivia. Many public and quasi-public enterprises in other countries have at some time shared the problems of COMIBOL: a lack of clearly defined objectives, excessive government interference in day-to-day operations, and being treated as "milch cows" to benefit other sectors. Those familiar with the political framework within which COMIBOL operates, and with its self-perception as a provider of social benefits, would agree that it is unrealistic to assume that COMIBOL can do away with its social objectives and functions in the foreseeable future. Thus it is futile to recommend changes involving the conversion of COMIBOL into a purely commercial enterprise whereby it is divested of all its social activities. Instead, ways must be found of making the performance of the corporation more efficient within its given framework. In this context, many improvements can be made in the performance of COMIBOL without radical changes of direction. In the following paragraphs, some such changes are discussed; these should not be seen as a comprehensive catalog of recommendations but as illustrative suggestions.

Table 25. *COMIBOL's Total Debt Outstanding and Disbursed, End 1982*
(US$ million)

	External debt
Bilateral	*6.617*
U.S. PL 480	1.823
United Kingdom	0.380
Austria	0.691
South Africa (Independent Development Corporation)	3.723
Multilateral	*0.107*
Andean Development Corporation (CAF)	0.107
Commercial banks	*61.363*
Comp. Luxemburgoise	0.800
First National City Bank	6.171
Manufacturers Hanover Trust	21.389
Skandinaviska Enskilda Bank	9.244
Marine Midland Bank	1.836
Libra Bank	3.600
S.F.E. Banking Corp.	16.000
Mercator, Panama	2.323
Suppliers	*15.084*
Vielle Montagne	0.434
Assoc. Casas Prefab. Puttalo (Finland)	0.353
Soviet Union	14.297
Other	*67.646*
Casas Prefab. Camea	0.445
Credito Gobierno Argentino	42.500
Credito Fomento (Ex-Indef.)	24.701
Subtotal external debt	*150.817*

	Domestic debt
Credito Consolidado 8-80	21.357
Casas Prefab. (Pizarreno y Dalmati)	0.136
Credito Soporte Financiero 4-81	106.000
Subtotal domestic debt	*127.493*
Total debt (external and domestic)	*278.310*

Source: Central Bank of Bolivia.

Some studies have predicted that, if COMIBOL continues to operate as at present, by the end of the five-year period terminating in 1986, it will have incurred an accumulated operating deficit of more than US$700 million.[5] While these projections may be excessively pessimistic, there is no doubt that the present financial position of COMIBOL is very grave, and in the absence of corrective measures it could become unmanageable. Improvements in the financial situation can be made both by reducing costs and increasing revenues.

Cost reductions can be effected through stricter control of overtime pay (reducing it gradually from about 25 percent of basic pay to about 10 percent); better controls to reduce theft of machinery and minerals; and minor cost reductions in the La Paz and Oruro offices. In view of the experience of La Palca, plans for the Machacamarca volatilization plant should be postponed until its economic feasibility has been established.[6] The infrastructure at Machacamarca should be used to convert it into the central warehouse. The present location of the warehouse in the center of Oruro results in excessive losses and transport costs. Machacamarca is much more convenient to most mines and is on the main railroad. With regard to transport, an effort should be made to reduce the number of makes of wagons, so that there are fewer spare parts shops. COMIBOL should also investigate the feasibility of transporting concentrates in large reusable plastic bags instead of in open wagons or bags of 40 kilograms, which would eliminate losses en route. But as yet no sound case exists for closing the railroad company, Ferrocorp; the social costs would be high, and the corporation would need to invest in a fleet of new wagons at a time of severe financial constraints.

The Unificada and Kami mines purchase substantial amounts of tin ores from cooperatives. The prices paid to the cooperatives leave COMIBOL with considerable losses on these purchases after taxes and selling costs. COMIBOL should negotiate a price that at least enables it to break even. COMIBOL can also reduce penalty and noncompliance of quality deductions on its concentrates by setting up central warehouses to receive all concentrates where these can be mixed in the proportions desired by ENAF or foreign smelters.

COMIBOL should undertake a detailed study of how to reduce operating costs in the provision of social services in those mines (Catavi, Unificada, Kami, Corocoro, Morococala, and Santa Fe) which can be expected to remain a financial drain on COMIBOL. Workers who are eligible for retirement, or who opt for retirement under some voluntary scheme, should be retired and not replaced. Some personnel should be reallocated to other mines. The government might designate certain mines as social necessities and pay COMIBOL an explicit subsidy to keep them operating. COMIBOL should continue to administer its educational, housing, and health programs since there is little guarantee that other public agencies would perform these services better. These activities, however, should be "costed out" and the cost of the programs should be kept separately and presented to the policymakers. This will ensure that the social costs and public interest arguments do not become an excuse for bad management and inefficiency. The prices of the four basic subsidized items, frozen since 1956, should be revised to more realistic levels to reduce the commissary losses of COMIBOL.

The government should examine the possibility of passing on to COMIBOL the benefits from refinancing COMIBOL's external debt.[7] If this is not possible, the domestic debt with the Central Bank should be refinanced. In practice, this is already happening. COMIBOL should continue to pay taxes to the Treasury (after adjustment for the social services provided) but the presumed costs should be indexed to actual changes in Bolivian mining costs. This will ensure more realistic levels of tax payments and a more rational tax structure (for details, see Chapter 7).

A relatively effortless way of obtaining revenue inflows in the short run would be to sell the obsolete and unnecessary machinery, materials, and spare parts stored in the central warehouses of Oruro. COMIBOL should obtain the legal clearance for selling these at prices as close as possible to current market prices. This could bring in about US$7 million in revenues.

COMIBOL can also obtain better prices on its commercial contracts, especially on "spot" sales, if the lengthy procedures for making these sales are simplified and if more authority, within certain financial limits, is given to the sales manager.

The above measures, together with new external financing, would probably enable COMIBOL to undertake a program of badly needed investment. The required investment over the next four to five years can be divided into (1) a short-term program for urgently needed investment to maintain present production and to undertake projects with low capital requirements and short gestation periods and (2) a long-term program for the completion of projects initiated in the first phase.

The main components of the short-term investment program would include: (1) initiating regional and on-property exploration, without which COMIBOL's future could be jeopardized. The areas of high probability for regional exploration are Japo-Maracocola and alluvial deposits of Carmen, Centenario, and Rio Beni; on-property exploration could begin in Bolivar, Huanuni, and Los Lipez; (2) undertaking projects with short gestation periods and requiring relatively low capital investment, such as the tailings projects, especially at Catavi, Huanuni, and Colquiri; (3) initiating the first phase of the development of the Bolivar mine to include exploration, development, and construction of a new mill; (4) increasing gradually the hoisting capacity at Colquiri, Huanuni,

Bolivar, San Jose, and Unificada mines; (5) starting a program of maintenance and equipment replacement, which would begin with in-depth studies of the needs of the various mines and priority replacement or acquisition of the necessary items; (6) initiating improvements in the safety program; and (7) improving the manufacture of spare parts by COMIBOL.

The long-term investment program would basically be a continuation of the work initiated, with the addition of exploration and development at Viloco and Caracoles. Some of COMIBOL's larger projects, such as the Bolivar project, can easily attract foreign loans or equity financing. Because of the present scarcity of foreign funds to Bolivia, the government may wish to study the various available alternatives for private, and for foreign, participation. Some such available alternatives are mentioned in Appendix C.

It is estimated that, if the first phase of the investment program is initiated by the end of 1985, by 1987 annual incremental tin production would amount to about 3,000 metric tons. A price for tin of US$7 a pound in 1987 would imply new foreign exchange earnings of about US$50 million in that year.

Some organizational and administrative changes can also be made without a major overhaul of the system. In Bolivia, as in many other developing countries, it is believed that intervention in the daily operations of public enterprises increases their accountability. Experience in COMIBOL has shown, however, that the reverse is true: excessive interference by the interventores of the Auditor General's Office in the operations of the mining enterprises and the overcentralization of functions in the La Paz and Oruro offices have left the mine managers with little enthusiasm and given them ample room to blame poor performance on others. It has also made them excessively conservative in an environment in which the rewards for success are small and the penalties for failure are high. There is urgent need, therefore, for delegating more power to the mine managers and for working out a simple system of key indicators by which their financial performance is examined periodically by the La Paz office. The complicated bidding and procurement procedures should also be simplified. At the same time, the present bonus system should be changed to make it more productivity oriented.

Available evidence suggests that the more government authorities confine their activities to explicit goal-setting and the less they interfere in the detailed operations of management, the higher the level of efficiency likely to be achieved.[8] Partly as a response to the desire to achieve the flexibility and initiative of the private sector, while still enjoying the powers of the state, the idea of converting COMIBOL into a true "holding company" of the Italian type has been suggested on occasion. But legal framework is one thing and actual operations quite another. In the Italian case, there was a genuine devolution of power from the government to the holding company. It is difficult to believe that this will occur in the case of COMIBOL in the foreseeable future. Without genuine devolution, efforts to establish the legal framework of a holding company in COMIBOL would only create a confused authority structure and aggravate the present problems.

Finally, the big unknown in the future of COMIBOL is the role of majority worker participation (*cogestión mayoritaria*) in the board of directors of COMIBOL. As already mentioned, the direct involvement of the representatives of mine workers in policy decisions can have a positive effect on labor productivity and discipline. But it can also work in the other direction, by politicizing COMIBOL to such a degree that its decisionmaking powers are paralyzed. Only time will tell the results of this interesting experiment.

Notes

1. For additional details on the problems of COMIBOL, see Price Waterhouse Associates, "COMIBOL: Diagnostico y Plan de Rehabilitación," a study done for the World Bank/United Nations Development Programme, 1982.

2. Another important factor affecting not only COMIBOL but also the rest of the mining sector is the exchange rate. This issue has already been discussed in Chapter 2.

3. The Operations Division is responsible for production from all the mining enterprises. It is also responsible for all centralized support services pertaining to metallurgy, geology, miners' cooperatives, and industrial safety and hygiene. The Auxiliary Engineering unit consists mainly of repair and maintenance and manufacture of some spare parts.

4. Of course, exploration expenditures in Bolivia can be expected to be somewhat lower than, say, in the United States and Canada, which have been more thoroughly explored, and new mines are becoming more difficult to find. But even compared with mining companies in other developing countries, COMIBOL's exploration expenditures are relatively low in relation to gross mineral sales. See Rex Bosson and Bension Varon, *The Mining Industry and the Developing Countries* (New York: Oxford University Press, 1977).

5. See, for example, Price Waterhouse Associates, "COMIBOL, Diagnostico y Plan de Rehabilitación," a study done for the World Bank/UNDP, 1982.

6. For a discussion of the problems of the La Palca volatilization plant, see Appendix D.

7. Currently all public entities whose external debt was renegotiated by the government with external lenders continue to pay the Central Bank on the original schedules.

8. For an interesting discussion of related issues, see Armeane M. Choksi, *State Intervention in the Industrialization of Developing Countries: Selected Issues*, World Bank Staff Working Paper no. 341 (Washington, D.C., 1979).

CHAPTER 6

Tin Smelting in Bolivia

For decades Bolivia has cherished the ambition of smelting its ores domestically. Scattered attempts to start smelting operations in the country go as far back as the First World War. In 1916 the South American Electric Smelting Company was set up, but electric smelting in Bolivia did not prove successful. During the war, when it became impossible to secure jute sacks for exporting tin concentrate, a certain Luis Soux smelted his own concentrates in Potosi, using *yareta* (a local plant) and *taquía* (llama dung) as fuel; he had some success in selling his tin on the Argentine market. This, however, was a small-scale operation, involving about a thousand tons of metallic tin a year. Writing in 1928, Marsh opinioned: "Smelting in Bolivia is out of the question at present," and she presented as reasons the lack of coal, the virtual nonexistence of hydroelectric power, and the high transport costs, which made it impossible to operate smelters profitably at some central point where the output of the scattered mines could be sent for reduction.[1] Other reasons propounded by various commentators have been the lack of oxygen needed for the smelter furnaces at the high altitudes of the Bolivian altiplano and the resultant "deration" of all machinery—roughly 30 percent of power loss is encountered.

Smelting and refining activities are at present almost entirely carried out by the state-owned National Smelting Company (Empresa Nacional de Fundiciones, ENAF), which was formed in 1966.[2] There are, however, a few privately owned tin smelters, and COMIBOL operates some tin volatilization plants.

In the 1940s and 1950s various pioneers started small smelting plants. The most noteworthy was the high-grade tin smelter at Oruro owned by Mariano Pero. Using local raw materials, his smelter had an initial capacity of 5,000 metric tons a year. Some of its concentrate feed came from Pero's Chojnacota mines. When supplies from other mines increased, Pero raised the capacity of the smelter to 10,000 tons a year. Undoubtedly, much of his success was due to the high grade of the concentrates, which had an average tin content of about 48 percent.

Another pioneer, the Ukranian-born Jorge Zalesky, carried out a series of metallurgical experiments in the laboratories of Banco Minero de Bolivia with the intent of proving that smelting in Bolivia was a technically feasible proposition. He set up a low-grade tin smelter, Hormet, in Achachicala near La Paz. Zalesky was killed by a stray bullet during a civil disturbance (though how stray the bullet was has been a matter of great conjecture in Bolivia—many Bolivians were convinced that Zalesky knew too much about smelting to be acceptable to the international smelting interests). Despite severe financial problems and the death of Zalesky, the tin smelters of both Pero and Zalesky continue in operation to this day, although on a much reduced scale.

COMIBOL also operates a few small tin volatization plants (pyrometallurgical plants that convert low-grade or colloidal concentrates into more commercially suitable grades). In 1982, with assistance from the Soviet Union, COMIBOL completed the large volatilization plant of La Palca, near Potosí. The original investment was estimated at about US$8 million and the planned completion date was 1977. The actual cost, after a series of natural disasters and poor planning, was US$80 million.[3] Despite the unfortunate experience of La Palca, the government is planning to set up a similar but much larger plant at Machacamarca, near Oruro. The country may need to assess in detail the performance of the first plant before authorizing the construction of any further such plants.

In 1953 the government contracted the services of Krupp-Lurgi to prepare a feasibility study for a smelting plant. The study's conclusion was against such a plant on technical grounds. As a result of a pervasive feeling in Bolivia of a conspiracy by foreign owners of smelting plants to oppose domestic smelting in the country, and despite lingering doubts about the financial and technical feasibility of the project, the government of Bolivia signed an agreement on October 5, 1969, with Klockner for the first phase of the tin smelter. The smelter was to have a capacity of 7,500 metric tons a year for high-grade ores. The smelter, located at Vinto, seven kilometers from Oruro, was built in 1970 and became operational in early 1971. The process is conventional and consists of roasting concentrates to remove arsenic and antimony, followed by smelting with charcoal and suitable flux in two reverberatory furnaces. The crude tin metal so produced is thermally refined in cast iron kettles to a purity of 99.5 percent. The thermally refined tin is then cast into anodes and electrolytically refined to a purity of better than 99.9 percent.

In 1975 Klockner completed the expansion of this high grade smelter to 11,500 metric tons a year. The next expansion to 20,000 metric tons a year was carried out by Klockner in association with Paul Bergsoe and Sons of Denmark and was completed in 1977. This high-grade smelter receives all the concentrates that formerly went to Williams Harvey.

Finally, a new smelting plant for treating low-grade and complex tin concentrates with a capacity of 10,000 metric tons a year was completed in 1980. This raised the total smelting capacity to 30,000 tons a year, which constituted all of Bolivia's tin production. The low-grade smelter receives the concentrates that formerly went to Capper Pass and Metalgesellschaft.

Main Objectives of Tin Smelting in Bolivia

A number of arguments have been put forward by successive Bolivian governments in support of its forward-integration strategy in the mining sector. First, it has been argued that the net value added from the combined mining and metallurgical sector would be enhanced; transport, smelting, and insurance costs incurred abroad reduced; and net export receipts and fiscal revenues increased. Second, exporting metals instead of concentrates would broaden markets and Bolivia's sales would no longer be restricted to a small number of refineries and metal traders. Third, some minor employment would be created. Finally, a basis would be laid for establishing industries to process non-ferrous metals into plate, wire, and rods.

These objectives need to be analyzed in some detail. While there is no doubt that a shift to exporting refined metals instead of concentrates would increase net export earnings by reducing transport costs and eliminating most foreign refining fees, smelting operations normally generate low value added. As can be seen from Table 26, value added from the metallurgical sector accounted for only about 0.6 percent of total GDP by 1980, despite sizable investments in the sector during the 1970s.

Table 26. *Value Added in Mining and Metallurgy, 1970–80*
(US$ millions)

Value added ⸱	1970	1975	1978	1980
Mining value added	97.2	159.3	303.6	393.8
Metallurgy value added	0.2	6.0	23.0	34.2
Total GDP	1,041.6	2,473.1	4,030.0	5,980.2
Metallurgy value added as percentage of total GDP	0.02	0.24	0.57	0.57

Source: Central Bank of Bolivia.

56

These minor gains from expanded smelting have to be weighed against the forgone benefits from a correspondingly higher investment in mining or some other productive sectors of the economy. As regards market conditions, metal markets are indeed broader than those for unrefined minerals but they are also more complicated. Evidence of this is Bolivia's continued dependence on metal trading firms.[4] Moreover, most developed countries levy higher import duties on metals than on concentrates, and thus mineral-producing countries can expect lower net gains from a shift to metal exports. In terms of investment, since smelting projects typically have to be large scale to be economic, they require substantial (mostly foreign) capital, long gestation periods, and a level of coordination of various activities that is rare in most developing countries. Finally, while capital outlays for forward integration into semimanufactures and other metal products are not large, the domestic and even the Andean market is probably too small to allow economically feasible operations without heavy protection. The experience of Thailand with tinplate would seem to weigh against Bolivia's entering this activity.

In summary, while forward integration into smelting has its advantages, it is by no means an unmixed blessing. Any future investments must, therefore, be undertaken in the overall context of the Bolivian economy.

Performance of ENAF

With regard to the actual performance of ENAF's tin smelters, it is difficult to say that the objectives of the government have been achieved.[5] As can be seen from Table 27, capacity utilization has averaged less than two-thirds since the installation of the low-grade plant in 1980. The reasons for this low utilization rate are provided in subsequent paragraphs.

Table 28 provides the financial accounts of ENAF for the period 1973–82. As can be seen, the enterprise has experienced a deficit even on the current account for every year except 1979. The unfinanced part of the deficits has been normally covered by Central Bank financing.

On all accounts, the performance of ENAF has been one of unmitigated failure and a good example of how the achievement of a set of reasonable and realistic objectives can be frustrated by mismanagement, poor planning, lack of coordination, and technical and industrial relations problems. It is useful to recount some of the factors behind this performance.

Table 27. *Production of Metallic Tin by ENAF, 1971–82*
(fine metric tons)

Year	Production	Installed capacity	Capacity utilization (percent)
1971	6,969	7,500	92.9
1972	6,227	7,500	83.0
1973	6,954	7,500	92.7
1974	7,092	7,500	94.6
1975[a]	7,430	7,500	99.1
1976	9,185	11,500	79.9
1977[b]	12,786	20,000	63.9
1978	16,184	20,000	80.9
1979	15,696	20,000	78.5
1980[c]	17,863	30,000	59.5
1981	19,860	30,000	66.2
1982	19,463	30,000	64.9

a. Operation of new capacity started at the end of 1975.
b. Operation of new capacity started in June 1977.
c. Operation of low-grade concentrate began in April 1980.
Source: ENAF.

Table 28. *Revenues and Expenditures of ENAF, 1973–82*
(US$ millions)

Revenues and expenditures	1973	1974	1975	1976	1977	1978	1979	1980	1981	1982
Current revenues	32.3	59.3	51.3	73.8	138.6	211.7	245.6	211.1	274.7	274.6
Sale of goods and services	32.2	58.9	51.3	73.8	138.6	211.7	245.6	211.1	274.0	273.8
Other	0.1	0.4	0.0	0.0	0.0	0.0	0.0	0.0	0.7	0.8
Current expenditures	38.2	61.1	54.1	76.9	139.5	216.1	242.4	314.6	269.5	316.3
Labor costs	0.5	1.0	0.7	1.9	2.8	2.9	3.1	9.0	9.7	9.1
Purchase of goods and services	36.0	58.3	51.3	66.7	126.2	200.7	226.3	288.2	244.9	237.7
Interest payments	0.5	0.8	0.9	5.2	4.3	8.0	6.1	11.5	13.1	44.5
Internal debt	0.1	0.1	0.6	1.5	1.1	3.6	4.0	5.9	7.5	14.6
External debt	0.4	0.7	0.3	3.7	3.2	4.4	2.1	5.6	5.6	29.9
Other	1.2	1.0	1.2	3.1	6.2	4.5	6.9	5.9	1.8	25.0
Current account surplus or deficit(−)	−5.9	−1.8	−2.8	−3.2	−0.9	−4.4	3.2	−103.5	5.2	−41.7
Capital expenditures	0.3	32.5	15.4	20.5	62.7	3.9	32.3	20.4	2.0	2.2
Overall surplus or deficit (−)	−6.2	−34.3	−18.2	−23.7	−63.6	−8.3	−29.1	−123.9	−7.2	−43.9
Financing	6.2	34.3	18.2	23.7	63.6	8.3	29.1	123.9	7.2	43.9
External borrowing (net)	4.2	17.4	7.2	8.2	−2.2	−2.8	−9.9	17.3	−19.5	−10.2
Disbursements	4.2	17.4	8.3	9.8	—	3.1	0.3	23.5	2.9	0.0
Amortization	0.0	0.0	−1.1	−1.6	−2.2	−5.9	−10.2	−6.2	−22.4	−10.2
Domestic borrowing (net)	2.9	3.0	4.4	5.8	13.3	−2.5	−3.3	14.6	5.8	−15.8
Disbursements	4.1	4.2	5.4	6.6	15.5	1.7	4.1	17.4	7.8	—
Amortization	−1.2	−1.2	−1.0	−0.8	−2.2	−4.2	−7.4	−2.8	−2.0	−15.8
Short-term financing and cash balances	−0.9	13.9	6.6	9.7	52.5	13.6	42.3	92.0	20.9	69.9

Sources: ENAF; Central Bank of Bolivia.

ENAF's high-grade smelter was designed for an ultimate annual capacity of 20,000 fine metric tons of tin. Although production began in 1971 with initial capacity of 7,500 fine metric tons, the electric power, buildings, and other infrastructure for 20,000 fine metric tons had already been built. Also, there are no significant accessible coal deposits in Bolivia.[6] Instead, ENAF must use charcoal, which comes from domestic timber. From the very beginning, therefore, ENAF's smelting operations were costly.

Technically, the high-grade smelter has not encountered too many problems, although the machinery has been run down prematurely because of improper maintenance and large variations in the composition of fuel oil and other inputs. Also, an explosion in the volatilization furnace of the smelter closed it down for more than two months in 1980–81, and caused a loss of about US$5.5 million. Finally, production of metal in the high-grade smelter had to be reduced in 1981 and 1982 because some of its units had to produce pellets. These units were required to begin operations of the low-grade plant, because of delay in the start-up of operations of COMIBOL's La Palca volatilization plant. The major technical problems exist in the low-grade smelter, whose capacity utilization rate has never exceeded 30 percent. The main technical problem is in the exhaust system of the electric furnace, where an inadequate cooling system has done severe damage. The problem could have been avoided if tests had been carried out before the commencement of operations of the smelter. Moreover, according to the original plans, of the total feed received by the low-grade plant, only 29 percent would be in the form of tin oxide pellets from the volatilization plant at La Palca. But, since COMIBOL has been using a sizable portion of its own low-grade concentrates to convert them into pellets at La Palca (instead of supplying them to the low-grade smelter of ENAF), the latter has had to contend with a mixture of feed which is about 50 percent pellets. This mix has caused some problems in the reduction and refining section of the smelter, especially because of the presence of antimony in the pellets.

Table 29. *Price (c.i.f. Oruro) of Major Inputs of ENAF, 1977–82*
(U.S. dollars)

Inputs	1977	1978	1979	1980	1981	1982[a]
Domestic						
Cloth for filtration pipes (meter)	10.25	10.38	12.89	12.31	12.80	8.25
Pyrite (ton)	3.62	2.99	5.15	5.17	4.40	2.13
Sulphuric acid (ton)	94.44	99.41	99.63	243.19	368.00	1,013.50
Hydrocloric acid (ton)	618.00	642.99	678.02	742.14	905.00	812.50
Joiner's glue (ton)	0	1,200.00	1,205.95	2,159.77	2,404.80	2,966.25
Sulphur (ton)	135.50	111.37	107.84	170.65	161.60	147.38
Slack lime (ton)	74.29	93.93	110.35	128.48	145.20	103.94
Charcoal (ton)	90.60	95.75	96.96	128.50	165.60	117.75
Fuel oil (liter)	0.05	0.05	0.06	0.16	0.22	0.16
Imported						
Cresilic acid (ton)	1,423.02	925.52	907.38	1,467.82	2,106.40	2,422.36
Phenol sulphonic acid (ton)	545.46	576.40	564.24	1,070.84	1,346.40	1,481.04
Sodium carbonate (ton)	229.51	229.51	375.16	410.41	471.97	519.20
Caustic soda (ton)	0	358.30	302.25	652.95	685.60	767.86
Metallic magnesium (ton)	5,315.94	5,315.94	6,722.79	4,716.49	4,848.40	4,160.00
Metallic zinc (ton)	1,233.55	1,233.55	1,456.99	1,188.90	1,124.80	1,158.50
Amorphous carbon electrodes (piece)	0	0	0	2,134.14	0	0
Graphite electrodes (piece)	82.14	116.72	124.40	125.49	128.00	142.50
Bars (AKC) (piece)	514.30	514.30	426.57	446.29	397.02	405.80
Firebrick (ton)	1,296.90	1,296.69	1,221.60	1,271.26	3,836.50	1,198.91

a. The decline in per unit costs of domestic inputs (in U.S. dollars) in 1982 reflects the devaluation of the currency from US$1 = 25 pesos at the beginning of the year, to US$1 = 196 pesos at the end of the year. The average exchange rate for the year was US$1 = 80 pesos.

Source: ENAF.

In various reports of ENAF, frequent reference is made to a lack of spare parts and raw materials as a factor external to the enterprise. ENAF has frequently experienced shortages of fuel oil, charcoal, iron and cement for construction, and sulphuric acid, for example. But, more often than not, the lack of inputs has been a reflection of poor forward planning and administrative problems of ENAF rather than of the physical absence in the country of those parts and materials. The problem has been aggravated by excessively stringent and time-consuming procedures for bidding and procurement to which ENAF and other public agencies are subjected.

Another complaint generally heard in ENAF is the large increase in the prices of raw materials, both domestic and imported. Nevertheless, Table 29 demonstrates that only some of the materials have encountered significant increases (in U.S. dollar terms) in per unit costs of, say, more than 50 percent over the five-year period 1977–82. These include sulphuric acid, joiner's glue for woodwork, fuel oil (all domestic inputs), cresilic acid, phenol sulphonic acid, sodium carbonate, caustic soda and graphite electrodes (all imported). Increases in prices of inputs have not been a significant factor in the deterioration of ENAF's performance.

Labor costs, by constrast, rose much more rapidly. In 1978 ENAF had a wage bill of approximately US$3.9 million for a labor force of about 1,400 employees in tin smelting. By 1981, after the initiation of operations of the low-grade smelter, the wage bill had increased to more than US$8.6 million for 1,804 employees.[7] This implies that the average wage had increased by more than 70 percent in a period of three years.

From the very beginning ENAF has had to contend with a heavy debt burden. At the end of 1982 its external debt still outstanding amounted to about US$25.5 million, and domestic debt outstanding amounted to US$118 million (see Tables 30 and 31). Payments on these loans are a

Table 30. *External Debt of ENAF*
(US$ millions)

Lender	Original amount	Amount outstanding		Payments due in 1983		
		end 1980	end 1982	Interest	Amortization	Total
High-grade tin smelter						
Government of Denmark	1.136	0.915	0.757	0	0.063	0.063
Andean Development Corporation	2.208	1.528	1.052	0.081	0.271	0.352
Kreditanstalt Fur Wiederaufbau	15.275	15.274	0	0.763	0	0.763
Deutsche Sudamerikanische	4.200	0	0	0	0	0
Subtotal	22.819	17.717	1.809	0.844	0.334	1.178
Low-grade tin smelter						
Andean Development Corporation	4.500	4.158	3.377	0.296	0.446	0.742
Paul Bergsoe & Sons	4.160	3.813	2.080	1.135	0.693	0.828
Kreditanstalt Fur Wiederaufbau	10.452	9.837	7.378	0.548	1.230	1.778
Bank of America	4.000	4.000	3.273	0.553	0.800	1.353
Compagnie Luxembourgoise	22.239	16.220	5.167	0.579	2.067	2.646
Energomachexport	1.104	1.104	0.782	0.032	0.313	0.345
Machinexport	0.538	0.538	0.213	0.007	0.105	0.112
Licanzitorg	0.130	0.130	0.011	0.002	0.011	0.013
Subtotal	47.123	39.800	22.281	2.152	5.665	7.817
Antimony smelter						
Skodaexport	9.253	3.048	1.360	0.076	0.871	0.947
Subtotal	9.253	3.048	1.360	0.076	0.871	0.947
Total	79.195	60.565	25.450	3.072	6.870	9.942

a. Not included is a US$0.250 million loan from Davy Powergas for a fertilizer study, of which the amount outstanding at the end of 1982 was US$0.007 million.
Sources: Central Bank of Bolivia; ENAF.

Table 31. *Domestic Debt of ENAF*
(US$ millions)

Lender	Original amount	Amount outstanding		Payments due in 1983		
		end 1980	end 1982	Interest	Amortization	Total
Central Bank	128.815	55.443	118.070	10.628	1.195	11.823
Low-grade tin smelter	6.576	3.587	2.391	0.127	1.195	1.322
High-grade tin smelter	5.456	1.559	0.679	0.151	0	0.151
Antimony smelter	1.783	0.297	0	0	0	0
Revolving fund	115.000	50.000	115.000	10.350	0	10.350
INALPRE	0.280	0.280	0.170	0.011	0.089	0.100
Total	129.095	55.723	118.240	10.639	1.284	11.923

Sources: Central Bank of Bolivia; ENAF.

significant factor in ENAF's problems: in 1983, for example, the company had to pay about US$22 million in interest and amortization (foreign and domestic) payments.

Other factors have also aggravated the financial performance of ENAF. Strikes and work stoppages have been all too frequent, in some cases resulting in heavy losses in production. There is also an excess of labor, and managers in the company interviewed felt that ENAF could possibly produce more with half the present labor force. At the managerial level, ENAF suffers from the same syndrome that affects most public institutions in Bolivia, lack of continuity of senior staff. In the four-year period 1979–83, ENAF has had nine general managers. With such a short tenure, managers clearly cannot plan and schedule crucial activities seriously and are reluctant to make important decisions. ENAF also has encountered problems in the delivery of concentrates because of the production problems of COMIBOL. Other problems include the robbery of tin ingots, long delays in the shipment of the metal from the ports, and the failure of ENAF to obtain the best possible prices for the final product.[8]

Legally, COMIBOL and the private sector are constrained to sell all their concentrates to ENAF, and can export directly abroad only if the latter cannot smelt the concentrates. Smelting and other handling charges of ENAF are theoretically geared to fees charged by foreign smelters (Capper Pass in Britain for low-grade concentrates and Texas City in the United States for high-grade concentrates). When a producer sells to ENAF, therefore, the smelting and other charges are equivalent to charges abroad, plus nearly all of the transport cost savings from exporting metals instead of concentrates. But, as a result of the monopsonistic position of ENAF, with its concomitant inefficiencies, the smelting and other charges of ENAF have been, in practice, somewhat higher than those of foreign smelters, particularly since 1979. For illustrative purposes, two actual contracts for exactly the same concentrates for 1979 and 1983 are provided in Appendix E.

It is not surprising, therefore, that Bolivian producers of concentrates, both in the public and private sectors, are unanimous in their preference to export concentrates rather than to sell to ENAF. The treatment charges and penalties for impurities of ENAF are generally higher. The payment terms given by ENAF are unfavorable: COMIBOL and private companies are paid 80 percent of the value of the concentrates fifteen days after delivery and are charged interest on this amount until full payment about four months later. Moreover, since producers of concentrates began to sell to ENAF, they have lost access to invaluable foreign lines of credit from metal buyers.

One idea that has been discussed for some time in Bolivia, and which merits attention, is that of converting ENAF's operations into a "toll" system, whereby ENAF would charge the producers a fee for smelting and refining, but the ownership of the mineral would remain with the producers. This would ensure that, by concentrating solely on smelting and refining activities, ENAF's working capital requirements would be reduced. Its specialization in more limited activities would raise efficiency, and the producers would regain access to foreign credits.

Notes

1. Margaret A. Marsh, *The Bankers in Bolivia: A Study in American Foreign Investment* (New York: AMS Press, 1970).

2. The decrees which set up ENAF forbade the construction of new private smelters, but allowed the operations of those already established.

3. For a discussion of some of these problems, see Appendix D.

4. The main metal traders involved in Bolivian tin sales are Berisford Metals (Bolivia) Ltd., Marc Rich (Alpe), Philip Brothers, and Metall-Chemie. About a dozen others are involved in other metals and minerals.

5. Since 1976 ENAF also has in operation an antimony smelter, but this is not discussed here.

6. An anthracite type of coal deposit exists near Copacabana on Lake Titicaca, and less known indications of coal exist in the department of Cochabamba. These deposits, however, do not appear industrially exploitable at present.

7. Data for the antimony smelter are not included.

8. Under the present system, ENAF receives the lowest London Metal Exchange price quotation during a period of fifteen days before arrival of the metal at the port of destination and fifteen days after arrival. Also, ENAF's marketing outlets are inadequate, and the company ends up paying unnecessary agency fees.

CHAPTER 7

Issues and Policies Related
to Bolivian Mining Taxation

There are no fewer than twenty main types of taxes and more than thirty low-yield "earmarked" levies that affect the mining sector in Bolivia. For all practical purposes, the major mining taxes are assessed on gross value of exports and are considered equivalent to output taxes by the mining enterprises. Until March 1980 the two principal mineral taxes, accounting for 90 percent of mining tax revenues, were the *regalia* and the export tax.[1]

The regalia is a tax on "presumed income," which is the difference between world mineral prices in a specified market (namely the London Metal Exchange) and a presumed cost set by the government. The regalia is expressed in terms of taxes due for each "commercial unit" of the mineral in question. For such minerals as tin, copper, lead, and zinc, the commercial unit is the "fine pound" (*libra fina*). This is intended to represent the actual metallic content for each unit of the concentrate of metal exported. For other metals, such as antimony and wolfram, the commercial unit is the "long unit" (*unidad larga*) or 22.4 pounds of metallic content. The levels of presumed costs have been changed very infrequently in the past.

The export tax was imposed in October 1972 as a temporary levy to capture some of the windfall gains resulting from the devaluation in that year. Like many "emergency" fiscal measures elsewhere in the world, it remained an important fixture in the revenue structure until it was abolished in March 1980. Initially, the tax was 20 percent of net export values, but in October 1973 it was converted (primarily for administrative reasons) to a levy on gross values, and the nominal general rate was reduced to 7.5 percent or less on most mineral exports.

Drawbacks of the Present System

Overall, the level of mineral taxation in Bolivia has been one of the highest among the major tin-exporting countries. As can be seen from Table 32, the average joint burden of the regalia and the export tax has been equivalent to about 37 percent of gross tin revenues over the period 1970–81.

In addition, the structure of mining taxation in Bolivia has suffered from a number of serious drawbacks. First, the tax structure has adversely affected incentives for efficiency, exploration, and concentration, since the system has made the processing of low-grade ore unprofitable. It has led to inefficient use of concentrators because the taxes are based on the concentrates actually produced, not on the ore taken from the mine. Second, the tax regime has served to dampen incentives for both exploration and development because it does not take into account interenterprise cost variances of any kind, including exploration costs. Under the existing system, a mine that spends large sums on exploration and development pays the same taxes as a mine that spends none. The exploration incentive is further dampened by the low rates of land taxes (*patentes*) since it is profitable for individuals to hold large tracts of potentially rich land as unexploited reserves.

In March 1980 the government adopted several changes in mining taxation. The main features of the reform were (1) the elimination of the ad valorem export tax; (2) the updating of the presumed cost; and (3) the adoption of an adjustment mechanism that would allow for a more

Table 32. *Effective Rates of Regalia and Export Taxes for Tin, 1970–81*

Tax	1970	1971	1972	1973	1974	1975	1976	1977	1978	1979	1980	1981
Regalia payments (US$ millions)	50.3	23.1	30.6	42.2	85.8	61.2	71.5	103.0	118.9	139.5	117.5	93.3
Export tax payments (US$ millions)	0.0	0.0	7.7	15.8	24.0	16.4	16.3	18.8	26.6	22.3	1.3	0.0
Gross tin revenues (US$ millions)	102.0	105.9	113.5	131.0	230.1	180.0	228.1	328.8	373.7	395.6	378.1	343.1
Effective regalia rate (percent)	49.3	21.8	27.0	32.2	37.3	34.0	31.3	31.3	31.8	35.3	31.1	27.2
Effective export tax rate (percent)	0.0	0.0	6.8	12.1	10.4	9.1	7.1	5.7	7.1	5.6	0.3	0.0
Combined effect of both (percent)	49.3	21.8	33.8	44.4	47.7	40.1	38.4	37.0	38.9	40.9	31.4	27.2
Memorandum items												
Presumed cost (US$/lb) [a]	1.10	1.10	1.10	1.10	1.50	1.50	1.80	1.80	1.80	1.80	3.63	3.93
Average price of tin (US$/lb)	1.68	1.58	1.69	2.11	3.60	3.11	3.40	4.78	5.72	6.77	7.61	6.39

a. Changes in the presumed cost occurred in February 1974, January 1976, April 1980, and January 1981.
Sources: Ministry of Mining and Metallurgy; Ministry of Finance.

realistic (and more frequently adjusted) deduction of presumed costs from the taxable base. Under this system, the presumed costs would be updated in line with the floor price of the International Tin Council (ITC).

While the mining tax reform reduced the tax burden on the sector (the sector paid about US$30 million less in taxes than it would have paid without these measures) and while the principle of frequent adjustments of presumed costs was accepted, the major structural defects of the system remain. Moreover, the use of changes in the floor price of the ITC is less than satisfactory because that index is heavily influenced by changes in mining costs in Malaysia, the least-cost producer, and, as such, it would only be a matter of time before movements of actual mining costs in Bolivia would diverge from the movements of the ITC floor price.

Alternatives for Mineral Tax Reform

The present mining tax system in Bolivia is in need of reform to encourage more efficient and rational use of the existing capacity in the mining sector. A change in the tax structure would also encourage investment in the sector. Three major constraints, however, limit the range of feasible alternatives:

- The administrative machinery in the Ministry of Finance and the Ministry of Mining and Metallurgy is not adequate to implement immediately a highly ambitious once-and-for-all reform of mining taxes.
- The management and accounting infrastructure in the mining sector itself is not at present adequate to allow full compliance with the provisions of sophisticated mining tax legislation.
- Related to the administrative-compliance constraints above, and arising from the heavy governmental dependence on mineral taxes as a source of revenue, is the fear of significant loss of revenues in switching to a proportional income tax. Furthermore, the magnitude of such a loss under a pure income tax is virtually impossible to predict with any degree of precision.

Because of these constraints, there appear to be two basic alternatives for reform of mining taxation. The first is a true income or profits tax, which would clearly be superior in terms of improving efficiency and encouraging investment (domestic as well as foreign). The second alternative is an indexed regalia tax under which changes in presumed costs would be made in line with actual change in input costs. Such a tax would be superior on revenue grounds, at least in the short to medium term, and could be implemented quickly. It would also contribute to efficient use of existing capacity and would facilitate the expansion of investment in the sector (although to a much lesser extent than a true income tax).

A true income tax in the mining sector, therefore, represents the ideal toward which mining taxation in Bolivia should evolve. But, successful implementation of income taxation would require a more advanced tax administration and compliance infrastructure than is now present in Bolivia. A premature and hurried effort to install a true income tax on the mining sector might be worse than none at all. The country has already had one brief and unsatisfactory experience (1952–57) because of hasty implementation of net income taxes on mining. A carefully designed technical assistance program can succeed in creating, in rapid order, the kind of tax administration machinery capable of meeting the heavy demands inherent in the operation of income taxation of mining activities. But the caliber of the tax administration is only one side of the coin of effective taxation of mining profits. The compliance capacities of the principal mining enterprises must be considered as well. A comprehensive report on mining accounting was prepared in 1981 by the Canadian firm Woods Gordon (for the Canadian International Development Agency). It is generally agreed that about six private medium-size mining companies are in a position to implement the Woods Gordon system.

For these reasons it would be more appropriate to adopt indexation of presumed costs first and then shift to income taxation once the administration and compliance infrastructure is in place.

The principal features of the mining cost indexation system are:

- Standard mining costs for each mineral in the base period are calculated for each type of mine: COMIBOL, medium mines, small mines, and cooperatives.
- The standard mining cost is adjusted every six months, say, January and July, according to a Bolivian mining cost index.
- One national index is applied to adjust all standard mining costs through time.
- The cost index is a simple calculation dependent upon the Bolivian mining cost structure for its weights and inflation rates of main cost elements in Bolivian mining.
- The weights of the index are calculated every three years.
- The tax is determined as a percentage of the difference between the official price minus the actual nonmining costs, and the adjusted standard mining costs.

The automatic indexation system represents an improvement over the present mining taxation policies in five main ways. First, the semiannual revision of the standard mining cost by a Bolivian adjustment factor is bound to keep the presumptive cost in line with real mining costs. Second, the system will be sensitive to inflation rates and price increases and, therefore, will automatically adjust the tax burden accordingly, and reduce the burden of inflation on the mining sector. Third, it will reduce the disincentives on low-grade ore production by eliminating the nonmining costs from the tax calculation. Fourth, it will create a more stable environment for the mining enterprise with less risk of paying taxes of more than 100 percent of income. And fifth, immediately following a devaluation, while export taxes need to supplement the regalia under the present system, the proposed system will automatically increase the tax burden without the need for an extra tax on windfall profits.

The indexation system still leaves much to be desired. It does little to differentiate between variations in mining costs among enterprises, as would a pure income tax. It gives little incentive to investment in maintenance and repair, capacity expansion, or exploration and development. It does not fully exploit rents during periods of high mineral prices as would a graduated progressive tax system. It still presents disincentives for the mining of certain minerals because it does not change the arbitrariness of the tax rates on the different minerals. It should, therefore, be considered an interim measure.

Note

1. For a comprehensive discussion of mining taxation in Bolivia, see Malcolm Gillis and others, *Taxation and Mining: Nonfuel Minerals in Bolivia and Other Countries* (Cambridge, Mass.: Ballinger Publishing Company, 1978). This chapter draws on information from that publication.

CHAPTER 8

Prospects for Tin Mining
in Bolivia

The future of tin mining and metallurgical activities in Bolivia depends on two separate but related sets of factors: international market prospects for tin and domestic performance and policies in the tin sector of Bolivia. The first set of factors—medium- and long-term international prospects for tin—is one over which Bolivia can exercise little control, except through its indirect influence in the International Tin Council (ITC) and possibly through its role in the fledgling Association of Tin-Producing Countries.[1] By contrast, Bolivia has substantial control over domestic factors, namely the government's objectives for the sector, plans for the rehabilitation of the nationalized sector (especially for improved operational efficiency and more productive investments), exchange rate and tax policies, and credit availability.

International Market Prospects

The short-run prospects for tin are expected to be influenced primarily by the accumulated stocks which are at unprecedentedly high levels. The gap between global production and consumption of tin began to increase after 1978 (see Table 33 and Figure 7). In mid-1983, the London Metal

Table 33. *Tin Stocks*
(metric tons)

Year	Tin metal	Tin concentrates	Total
1965	44,700	10,000	55,494
1966	41,600	15,600	58,532
1967	45,500	12,430	66,435
1968	55,400	13,770	91,177
1969	42,100	11,210	62,379
1970	36,200	13,882	53,444
1971	39,200	10,600	63,496
1972	41,700	9,100	70,129
1973	38,200	12,200	53,981
1974	40,000	10,300	52,632
1975	43,500	15,700	86,496
1976	38,700	7,800	52,656
1977	35,900	8,400	48,385
1978	33,700	3,900	45,185
1979	28,000	11,200	40,940
1980	33,800	10,200	47,920
1981	42,100	9,300	70,135
1982	65,400	19,358	84,758
1983[a]	69,815	18,293	88,100

a. Preliminary.
Source: International Tin Council, *Tin Statistics*, various issues.

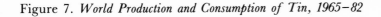

Figure 7. *World Production and Consumption of Tin, 1965–82*

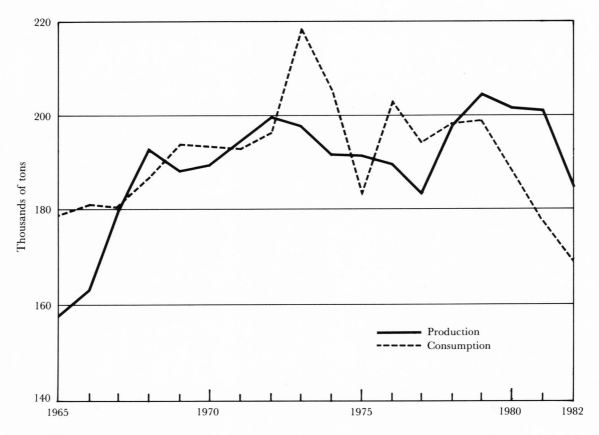

Note: Primary tin only. As for China and U.S.S.R., only exports and imports, instead of production and consumption, are included.

Source: International Tin Council, *Tin Statistics*, various issues.

Exchange had approximately 43,000 tons of tin metal in its warehouses. Moreover, because of the export controls exercised by the ITC since mid-1982, tin-exporting countries and traders have accumulated about 27,000 tons of tin metal and 18,000 tons of tin concentrates. As a result, the current stock level of about 88,000 tons is roughly 55 percent higher than the average during the 1970s.[2]

Under these circumstances, there will probably be persistent pressure on tin prices in the short term. The producing countries can be expected to react to this situation by cutting production, and, as in the past, this production cut will be effected through maintenance of the present shares of producing countries, rather than through outright ouster of the marginal producers. But the possibility cannot be ruled out that the ITC system will lose control over markets. In such an eventuality, the high-cost producers, such as Bolivia, will suffer most.

The demand for tin in the medium and long term will be affected to a large extent by the degree of substitution from other materials, especially from aluminum and plastics. Because of its favorable physical and chemical properties, such as extraordinary malleability, resistance to corrosion, lightness, nontoxity, easy conductivity, and antifriction qualities, tin has had a wide variety of uses over centuries. But the rate of growth of world tin consumption between 1930 and 1980 averaged only about 0.5 percent a year—lower than both its historical growth rate (tin consumption increased between 1.5 percent and 3.2 percent a year between 1800 and 1930) and the growth rate

Table 34. *Growth Rates of World Metal Consumption, 1961–80*
(annual percent)

Metal	1961–70	1970–80	1961–80
Tin	0.8	−0.3	0.3
Aluminum	9.8	4.6	7.1
Copper	4.0	2.9	3.4
Lead	4.0	2.5	3.4
Zinc	6.0	1.9	3.5
Steel	5.9	2.0	3.9

Note: Growth rates indicate least-squares trend.
Source: The World Bank.

of consumption for other metals (see Table 34). Interestingly enough, however, the price of tin increased almost consistently in relation to the price of other important metals (see Table 35). Over the past two decades tin has been the only major metal whose price has increased in real terms. This increase in the relative price of tin, particularly with respect to aluminum, is bound to have a far-reaching effect on demand for tin in the future. In fact, the use of tin for tinplate production, which constitutes the largest percentage share of tin consumption (see Table 36), has declined over the past decade; this has been partly due to substitution of aluminum and plastics for tin in can production, and partly due to technological advances in electrolytic processes, which have reduced the use of tin per square meter of tinplate. Tin for soldering is its second largest use, particularly in automobile radiators, in plumbing, and, most important, in electronic and domestic electrical

Table 35. *Price of Tin in Relation to Other Metals, 1800–1982*

Period	Aluminum	Copper	Lead	Zinc
1800[a]	n.a.	0.7	5.2	n.a.
1850[a]	n.a.	1.0	4.9	5.2
1900[a]	0.8	1.0	8.7	6.2
1930[a]	1.7	2.4	8.6	8.7
1950–54	6.2	3.7	7.2	7.2
1955–59	4.2	3.0	8.2	9.1
1960–64	5.1	3.7	13.2	11.0
1965–69	6.3	2.6	12.9	12.2
1970–74	6.8	3.2	12.8	7.8
1975–79	10.4	7.3	16.0	15.9
1980–82	10.6	8.2	20.7	17.4

Note: The price of the metal with which tin is compared is set at 1.0.
n.a. Not available.
a. Based on three-year averages.
Sources: For the period 1800–1930, C. J. Schmitz, *World Non-Ferrous Metal Production and Prices, 1700–1976*; for other years, the World Bank.

Table 36. *Percentage Share and Annual Growth Rate of Consumption of Tin Products, 1963–81*

Product	Percentage share		Annual growth rate (percent)		
	1963	1981	1963–69	1970–81	1963–81
Tinplate	40.2	35.4	−0.6	−2.6	−1.6
Tinning	4.5	4.6	−3.6	−1.4	−1.1
Solder	19.6	26.8	−1.2	−0.9	0.5
White metal, babbitt, and antifriction metal	7.7	8.7	−0.4	−1.0	0.6
Bronze and brass	14.3	7.5	−13.5	−2.4	−4.1
Other	13.7	17.0	−10.0	2.1	2.0
Total	100.0	100.0	−3.4	−1.3	−0.7

Note: Includes United States, United Kingdom, Federal Republic of Germany, France, Belgium, Italy, Netherlands, Switzerland, Austria, Japan, Australia, India, and Brazil.

goods. Although demand for tin for soldering has registered a gradual increase, and the electronics industry has shown a rapid growth rate, the tendency toward miniaturization of electronic products has reduced the use of tin for soldering. Perhaps the brightest prospects for tin are in its "other" uses, mainly new uses such as the production of chemical cans.

Within this context of low growth in the demand for tin, two scenarios are conceivable for the long term. In the first scenario, the current large tin producers are assumed to continue their control, however feeble, over the world markets. It is assumed that the intervention of the ITC, and probably of the Association of Tin-Producing Countries, will raise the level of tin prices to cover the production costs of present producers. There is evidence that by the late 1980s a number of on-shore, low-cost mines in Southeast Asia will have been depleted, and future operations may have to move to deeper seabeds. There is likely, therefore, to be strong pressure to retain the historical trend of real price increases, once the current problem of pending stock has been resolved. In such an eventuality, substitution will continue in all those activities, such as canning, where such possibilities exist.

The second scenario is one in which the control over world tin markets of the present producers is loosened gradually by the emergence of new producers. Brazil appears to be the most effective newcomer. In the early 1970s Brazil produced only 2,000 tons of tin a year; by 1981 its production had increased to 8,000 tons. At the present rate of increase, Brazil may well overtake Bolivia by the late 1980s. If Brazil's expansion stimulates present producers to increase production and to reduce prices, the most likely result could be the ousting of high-cost producers.

Domestic Considerations

Short-term prospects for increased output and improved productivity in Bolivian tin mining are not bright. Past neglect of exploration and mine development, the chaotic state of COMIBOL, the unresolved situation of workers' participation in the nationalized sector, lack of credit, as well as the present system of exchange rates, which discourages all exporting activities including mining, are some of the factors which could prevent a recovery of tin production from its estimated 1983 level of about 22,000 tons—the lowest level since the late 1950s and early 1960s.

A move to a more realistic exchange rate (and its maintenance thereafter), the adoption of a system of mining taxation that provides more incentives for investment, and greater access to foreign credits would ensure the recovery of the more dynamic medium-size mining sector from its present problems. Once a proper policy mix is in place, no other major constraints exist for the medium-size mining sector to increase capacity utilization from its present level of about 75 percent. Prospects for increased production are reasonably bright for the private mines of Milluni and Chojlla.

The problems of COMIBOL, however, are somewhat more intractable, and policy changes alone would not be sufficient to increase its productivity in the short run. The immediate years ahead should, therefore, be used to introduce the organizational, financial, and administrative changes mentioned in Chapter 5 to put COMIBOL on a sounder financial footing.

Even with a successful rehabilitation program for COMIBOL and with improved international prospects for tin, the problems of public sector tin mining in Bolivia can be expected to persist for a number of years. There are, however, some reasonably attractive projects in tailings treatment, especially at Catavi, Colquiri, Huanuni, and San Miguel. There are also possibilities in the Cordillera de Tres Cruces, La Meseta de Morococala, and the region of Tasna-Chorolque, provided exploration and mine development efforts are intensified. Another important project is the development of the Bolivar mine. But, at least in the first few years, increased production as a result of these new investments will almost completely be annulled by declining output of those mines where deposits have been progressively exhausted.

In short, even under the most optimistic scenario, prospects for tin mining in Bolivia appear dim, particularly in the public sector. Until the tin potential of the Bolivian lowlands is better assessed, it may be premature to suggest that the days of tin mining in that country are over. But there is little doubt that the most that can be done during the next several years is to maintain Bolivia's tin production at the present level. Meanwhile, an effort should be made to diversify gradually into other metals such as gold, silver, and zinc. On a macroeconomic basis, the share of overall mining activities in GDP can also be expected to decline as the hydrocarbons, agriculture, and agroindustrial sectors benefit from the trend toward diversification.

Notes

1. Bolivia has not signed the current (sixth) International Tin Agreement, which came into effect in June 1982. Nevetheless, it is a member of the Association of Tin-Producing Countries. The other members of this association are Malaysia, Indonesia, Thailand, Zaire, and Nigeria.

2. In addition, the U.S. General Services Administration (GSA) has approval for sales of 34,000 tons from its buffer stock. The recent agreement between the U.S. and Asian tin producers, however, limits annual sales to 3,000 tons.

APPENDIX A

List of Bolivian Mining Companies Included in the Survey

Medium-Size Mining Sector

Of the fifteen medium-size mining companies that produce tin, twelve were included in the survey. Two of them were not included because of difficulties of disaggregating their data for tin operations alone, and one of them had incomplete information. Of the twelve, the following ten produce only tin: Estalsa, Avicaya, Barrosquira, Cerro Grande, Suka, Soteca, Pabon, Orlandini, Atoroma, Somar, and Leque Chico. The remaining two produce other minerals in addition to tin. These are International Mining and Yana Mallcu.

COMIBOL

Of the fifteen main mining enterprises of COMIBOL, thirteen were included in the survey. The two excluded, Corocoro and Matilde, do not produce any tin. Of the thirteen, three (Catavi, Huanuni, and Santa Fe) produce only tin. The remaining ten produce tin in conjunction with other minerals. These are Quechisla, Colquiri, Unificada, San Jose, Caracoles, Viloco, Bolivar, Kami, Bolsa Negra, and Colquechaca. The proportion of tin in total mineral production varies considerably among these enterprises, ranging from about 95 percent for Colquiri and Caracoles to only about 5 percent for Kami and Bolivar.

APPENDIX B

Aggregated Sample Data for The Bolivian Tin-Mining Sector, 1980–81
(US$)

Costs	Medium mining		COMIBOL		Total sector	
	1980	1981	1980	1981	1980	1981
Total labor costs	12,279,657	13,142,713	57,855,351	75,715,348	70,135,008	88,858,061
Direct labor costs	9,432,036	8,031,337	26,708,311	28,533,561	36,140,347	36,564,898
Indirect labor costs	2,847,621	5,111,376	31,147,040	47,181,787	33,994,661	52,293,163
Family subsidies	233,456	10,854	1,202,025	2,183,857	1,435,481	2,194,711
Social expenses	1,429,486	3,389,026	14,259,601	18,644,632	15,689,087	22,033,658
Indemnifications	1,184,679	1,293,652	4,128,853	6,783,237	5,313,532	8,076,889
Perdida pulperias	0	417,844	11,556,561	19,570,061	11,556,561	19,987,905
Total material costs	4,866,013	5,886,045	20,346,032	25,391,746	25,212,045	31,277,791
Domestic material costs	1,229,305	1,391,901	4,218,144	5,119,274	5,337,449	6,511,175
Foreign material costs	3,746,708	4,494,144	16,127,888	20,272,472	19,874,596	24,766,616
Total energy costs	2,032,497	3,431,386	6,755,279	12,813,844	8,787,776	16,245,230
Electricity costs	1,492,523	2,211,417	4,605,279	9,533,883	6,097,802	11,745,300
Petroleum product costs	539,974	1,219,969	2,150,000	3,279,961	2,689,974	4,499,930
Transport costs	1,748,571	1,165,185	5,669,402	8,861,250	7,417,973	10,026,435
Smelting costs	12,699,015	13,477,447	40,749,273	44,142,837	53,448,288	57,620,284
Other costs	8,633,501	6,861,058	9,048,159	12,249,011	17,681,660	19,110,069
Depreciation expenses	3,539,940	2,917,588	4,779,084	5,629,541	8,391,024	8,547,129
Financial costs	4,087,899	4,214,994	12,294,523	16,021,891	16,382,422	20,236,885
Total costs before taxes	49,887,093	51,096,416	157,497,103	200,825,468	207,384,196	251,921,884
Taxes	18,085,068	13,461,464	57,483,176	33,699,030	75,568,244	47,160,494
Regalias	16,819,409	12,811,431	55,348,612	33,699,030	72,168,021	46,510,461
Export and other taxes	1,265,659	650,033	2,134,564	0	3,400,223	650,033
Total costs	67,972,161	64,557,880	214,980,279	234,524,498	282,952,440	299,082,378
Gross tin sales	71,239,917	62,526,532	236,876,704	215,931,230	308,116,621	278,457,762
Sales to ENAF	59,860,166	53,359,259	202,518,632	202,044,959	262,378,798	255,404,218
Sales abroad	11,379,751	9,167,273	34,358,072	13,886,271	45,737,823	23,053,544

APPENDIX C

Alternative Legal and Contractual Agreements for Mineral Development

An important consideration for a developing country and its mineral agencies is the legal and contractual arrangement selected for the development of specific mining projects. In principle, there is a wide spectrum of choices, with varying degrees of foreign participation. The purpose of this appendix is to describe the various alternatives available and to outline their advantages and disadvantages. Clearly, the ultimate choice will depend on factors such as political acceptability, the quality of domestic technical expertise, the profitability of the project, the stage of development of the mining deposit and the interest of foreign companies in participating in the project.

The main alternatives available, with increasing degree of foreign participation, are:

1. Unpackaged input from foreign sources, financed externally
2. Packaged input from foreign sources, financed externally—the turnkey approach
3. Cooperation with foreign companies on the basis of nonequity forms of risk-sharing and benefit sharing—the "association contract"
4. Cooperation with foreign companies on the basis of formal, equity-based corporate joint ventures
5. Divestiture by sales or competitive bidding to private (foreign or domestic) companies as holders of mining rights.

Unpackaged Purchase of Equipment and Services

The underlying assumption of this arrangement is that the domestic company will be responsible for the execution of the project. It will have to be purchaser and general contractor and coordinate individual purchase contracts. Foreign companies would only supply individual components of the project.

The advantage of this type of contract is that it places the onus of execution on the domestic company and provides, at least in principle, the opportunity for self-reliance. It also reduces the negative aspects of multinational corporations such as the misuse of transfer pricing, overpricing, and captive mine projects. The disadvantage of this type of agreement, however, is that it requires substantial coordination from the domestic company, without which the project may encounter long delays.

Packaged Purchase: the Turnkey Approach

Under this arrangement, packages of technology and equipment are purchased in the form of a turnkey contract (often complemented by postoperational technical assistance and even management obligations). A general contractor assumes the obligation to execute the project until production commences. The amount paid to the contractor generally includes the price of the separate components plus special fees as compensation for the general coordination and risk associated with completion and performance guarantees. Since the successful completion of a

Note: This appendix is based on Thomas Walde, "Mission Report on Bolivia," prepared for the U.N. Department of Technical Cooperation for Development (New York: March 1982), processed.

project under this arrangement depends largely on the quality of the selected contractor, serious attention should be given to choosing an appropriate contractor.

Several advantages exist in the use of turnkey arrangements. There is generally a greater assurance that the project will be completed on schedule. Experienced contractors can economize on costs from their knowledge of markets and their well-developed procurement systems. External financing will usually be more forthcoming than under the first alternative, because of the completion guarantees provided by, as well as the confidence in the technical capabilities of, the contractor. The main disadvantage is the higher price, which can be cut if the domestic company can undertake more coordination, as under the first alternative.

Association Contract: Project Cooperation with Shared Risks, Benefits, and Management on a Nonequity Basis

This arrangement provides for sharing of risks, benefits, and management without an explicit equity joint venture. The contract of association (also referred to as the "contract of mineral development cooperation" and "service-risk contract") has been employed effectively by Colombia in its dealings with large multinational companies. In Colombia, as in many other developing countries, constitutional and political exigencies made it more convenient to organize cooperation on a purely contractual basis, without giving the foreign partner any share in the mineral rights.

Under this arrangement, both parties contribute services in developing the mine and in managing the project. The national partner generally retains the supervisory and policymaking powers, whereas the foreign partner acts as a technical manager or adviser. Organizationally, there is typically a joint executive committee in which the state company has the majority but, important decisions require unanimity. Day-to-day management is left to the foreign partner, subject to the overall supervision of the domestic partner. Financially, a joint account is set up to which both parties contribute: the national company contributes generally through its mining rights and previous studies done, and the foreign partner contributes in cash or in kind. Should the project need greater capital contributions than available in the account, the foreign partner is obligated to advance funds (mostly as loans) on appropriate terms.

Once the project starts earning revenues, net proceeds are used first to repay loans and then to repay advances by the foreign partner. The remainder is split according to a contractually agreed percentage (say, 51:49 percent). Such revenue-sharing can be arranged on the basis of production-sharing. Provision can also be made to phase-out the foreign partner as national technical capabilities grow. For example, after a several years, the roles of technical manager or financial controller may revert to locals.

The association contract has several appealing features. Because mining rights are retained by the national company and no formalized corporate joint venture structure is established, there is less cause for political outcry. For the foreign partner, the system of revenue-sharing or production-sharing can be considerably attractive, particularly if it is linked to long-term supply contracts and rights of first refusal. National control is maintained through majority on the joint committees, while the foreign partner's concern for sound business management is taken into account through autonomy in day-to-day operations. Also, the phase-out provisions allow the national company to assume gradually full control over management. Foreign commercial banks will be more eager to provide financing to the extent that they trust the foreign partner's management capabilities. More important, these provisions force the foreign company to get more involved in the project. Under arrangements one and two (unpackaged purchase of equipment and services, and turnkey operations), the interest of the foreign supplier terminates with the completion of the project contract. In the case of association contracts (and the equity investment types discussed later), the foreign company's remuneration is based on profits. The ultimate success of the project (in terms of completion and production on schedule, economic and high-quality procurement, and effective training and management) is at the core of the foreign partner's interests. But because the involvement of the foreign partner is more intense than under the two previous schemes, it is more prone to political opposition.

Joint Equity Ventures

Joint equity ventures are used frequently in many developing countries where access to foreign capital, technology, managerial ability, and markets is an important consideration. It is also employed in some socialist countries such as China, Hungary, and Yugoslavia. Under this arrangement, a jointly owned company is set up. Shares of ownership or equity can change. The ownership ratio (50:50, 49:51, 75:25) is by no means indicative of the real division of benefits and control; ownership distribution can be circumvented by management contracts, management prerogatives, and rules on the composition of the board of directors. It is similar to the contract of association, but, whereas the contract of association uses contractual provisions to set up a cooperative relationship, the formal joint venture functions under corporate law.

The equity of the joint venture is contributed in cash or kind by the shareholders. Frequently, provision is made for government to contribute in the form of mining rights or profitable projects at the feasibility stage. The strategy should be to strike the right balance between the government's desire to maximize its participation and the foreign investors' desire for a reasonable rate of return on equity.

The organizational structure consists basically of the board of directors and the chief executive officers. The composition of the board normally reflects the distribution of equity capital. There have been instances, however, in which foreign partners have accepted government majority on the board even with government equity of only 25 percent.

A joint venture can be made more attractive if the foreign investor is able to obtain tax credit in his home country for taxes paid in the developing country. Often his rate of return calculations are greatly influenced—at no cost to the developing country—if some of his financial contributions are so formulated that foreign tax authorities consider them as taxes and allow tax credit.

Joint ventures have all the advantages of the association contract. In addition, external financing is generally even easier to arrange. Nevertheless, it may well be less acceptable politically in a number of countries.

Private Direct Investment

Fully privately owned investment to develop mines is an important option available to governments. It consists essentially of sale of deposits to private owners, who develop the projects. The government obtains revenues from the sale of mining rights and from taxes or other levies agreed upon.

A well-chosen private investor will generally be highly interested in the project's success, and noninterference from the state in the internal organization of the operating company may add another benefit. For the country, the arrangement implies saving on scarce skilled technical and managerial personnel.

The corresponding disadvantages are the lack of public control and accountability, possible misuse by investors of transfer pricing, and the use of inefficient and short-sighted mining practices ("creaming off"). But governments can control the activities of private enterprises in various ways. Reporting obligations to the government, obligations favoring national processing, rules on purchase of domestic inputs, use of national transport carriers, additional profit taxes, and compliance with state-issued directives on marketing and pricing are some examples.

APPENDIX D

Problems of La Palca Tin Volatilization Plant

During the early 1970s, the governments of Bolivia and the U.S.S.R. signed an agreement for the construction of a volatilization plant near Potosí. The initial cost was US$8.2 million. The plant was designed to produce 400 metric tons a day of 3 percent tin concentrates. This would produce about 3,500 metric tons a year of 50 percent tin concentrates at a scheduled on-stream time of eleven months out of twelve. The main source of concentrates was to be the Unificada mine at Potosí, where a new gravity preconcentration plant would be used to produce a 3 percent concentrate with 70 percent recovery. Although the tin concentrate to be obtained from the volatilization plant could be considered high grade by Bolivian standards, it would be too "dirty" to be processed in conventional smelters. The product would, therefore, be processed in the low-grade smelter of ENAF.

Civil works were initiated about a kilometer away from Potosí, and when these works were reasonably advanced, it was decided to change the site because of water shortages. La Palca, 15 kilometers from Potosí, was chosen, and civil works were again initiated, despite geological studies that cast doubts on the geological structure of the location. Because of landslides, the cost of civil works (initially estimated at about US$2 million) mounted to US$30 million.

The plant was completed ten years after initiation of construction, but before operations could begin, a portion of the plant caught fire, apparently because of faulty diesel burners.

A few days after start-up, the population of the region complained of heavy pollution from the plant. It was emitting an estimated 120 tons of sulphur a day, occasionally in the form of sulphuric acid, which did severe damage to plant and animal life in the region. Damages were paid and an area in the radius of one kilometer was bought. To overcome the problem, the sulphur content in the concentrates fed to the plant was reduced, and cool air was injected to disperse the fumes. When this did not work, a very tall chimney was built.

When normal operations resumed, titanium corrosion was detected in the chimney because of the presence of flourine and chlorine in some of the preconcentrates. The chimney had to be refurbished with a plastic material. Because of shortages of raw materials, the plant is now experiencing excess capacity.

As a result of all the aforementioned problems, the final cost of the investment was US$80 million, ten times the original estimated cost. The cost of production per ton treated is US$180 in 1982 prices.

APPENDIX E

Comparative Analysis of Terms and Conditions of Tin Concentrates Contracts, 1979
Specification: Sn 43%; As 0.12%; Sb. 0.06; S 2.0%; Fe 9.5%; Cu 0.02%; Pb 0.05%; Bi 0.3%; Zn 0.02%.
Price Quotation: Lowest price on LME: US$6,465 a fine metric ton.
Exchange Rate: £1 = US$1.9976.
Date: November 4, 1979.
(U.S. dollars a metric ton)

Value and deductions	Gulf Chemical	Capper Pass	Marc Rich	ENAF
Valuation				
Tin	5,904.25	5,986.20	5,914.94	5,894.99
Bonus	0.0	14.98	50.00	8.00
Total	5,904.25	6,001.18	5,964.94	5,902.99
Deductions				
Treatment charges	427.67	507.59	453.85	592.00
Contamination	0.0	33.74	0.0	0.0
Energy	0.0	68.32	0.0	80.23
Penalties	9.05	5.05	10.37	14.30
Realization costs	73.07	94.44	50.53	85.14
Financing	22.36	21.87	22.71	91.79
Weight loss	27.30	26.86	0.0	0.0
Total	559.45	757.87	537.46	863.46
Net payable to producer (a metric ton)	5,344.80	5,243.31	5,427.48	5,039.53

Comparative Analysis of Terms and Conditions of Tin Concentrates Contracts, 1983
Specification: Sn 39.87%; As 0.953%; Sb. 0.02%; S 6.235%; Fe 11.21%.
Price Quotation: Lowest price on LME: US$13,470 a fine metric ton.
Exchange Rate: £1 = US$1.4835.
Date: March 21, 1983.
(U.S. dollars a metric ton)

Value and deductions	Capper Pass	ENAF
Valuation		
Tin	5,235.90	5,235.90
Bonus	0.0	8.00
Total	5,235.90	5,235.90
Deductions		
Treatment charges	381.72	805.58
Contamination	38.81	0.0
Energy	183.18	0.0
Penalties	40.59	22.59
Realization costs	193.55	110.56
Financing	21.83	35.88
Weight loss	22.96	0.0
Total	882.64	974.61
Net payable to producer (a metric ton)	4,353.26	4,269.29

Statistical Appendix

CONTRIBUTION OF MINING TO THE BOLIVIAN ECONOMY

SA.1.	Share of Mining in Total GDP, 1970–80	*81*
SA.2.	Share of Mining in Total Labor Force, 1970–81	*81*
SA.3.	Contribution of Mining to Fiscal Revenues, 1970–81	*82*
SA.4.	Share of Mining in Total Merchandise Exports, 1970–82	*82*

DATA ON BOLIVIA'S LABOR FORCE

SA.5.	Share of Subsectors in Mining Labor Force, 1970–81	*83*
SA.6.	Employment in COMIBOL Mines, 1982	*83*

DATA ON BOLIVIA'S MINING FISCAL REVENUES

SA.7.	Composition of Mining Sector Revenues, 1970–81	*84*
SA.8.	Source of Regalia Payments, 1970–80	*84*
SA.9.	Source of Tin Regalia Payments, 1970–81	*85*
SA.10.	Source of Export Tax Payments, 1970–80	*85*

DATA ON BOLIVIA'S TIN PRODUCTION

SA.11.	Production of Tin Concentrates, 1973–82	*86*
SA.12.	Production of Metallic Tin, 1970–82	*86*
SA.13.	Bolivian and World Production of Tin Concentrates, 1900–82	*87*

DATA ON BOLIVIA'S EXPORTS OF TIN

SA.14.	Export Values of Tin Concentrates, 1970–82	*89*
SA.15.	Export Values of Metallic Tin, 1970–82	*89*

OTHER DATA ON BOLIVIAN MINING

SA.16.	Sales of Tin Concentrates to ENAF, 1973–81	*90*
SA.17.	Distribution of Medium–Size Mines by Fixed Assets, 1973–80	*90*
SA.18.	Distribution of Medium–Size Mines by Total Sales, 1973–80	*90*
SA.19.	Distribution of Medium–Size Mines by Profits, 1973–80	*91*
SA.20.	Distribution of Medium–Size Mines by Employment, 1974–80	*91*

DATA ON WORLD TIN MINING

SA.21.	World Production of Tin Concentrates, 1900–81	*92*
SA.22.	Rank of Major Producing Countries with Respect to Production of Tin Concentrates, 1960–82	*92*

SA.23. Production of Tin Metal   93

SA.24. Percentage Shares of Production by Economic Group, 1980   94

SA.25. Consumption of Tin Metal, 1950–81   94

SA.26. Annual Growth Rate of Tin Consumption by Product and Country, 1963–81   95

SA.27. Trade Flows of Tin Concentrates, 1965   96

SA.28. Trade Flows of Tin Metal, 1965   97

SA.29. Trade Flows of Tin Concentrates, 1970   98

SA.30. Trade Flows of Tin Metal, 1970   99

SA.31. Trade Flows of Tin Concentrates, 1975   100

SA.32. Trade Flows of Tin Metal, 1975   101

SA.33. Trade Flows of Tin Concentrates, 1981   102

SA.34. Trade Flows of Tin Metal, 1981   103

SA.35. Relative Prices of Tin with Respect to Other Major Metals, 1800–1982   104

SA.36. Price Indices of Tin, Aluminum, and Copper, 1950–82   104

Table SA.1. *Share of Mining in Total GDP, 1970–80*
(millions of Bolivian pesos, current prices)

Year	Total GDP	Mining value added[a]	Mining as a percentage of total GDP
1970	12,374	1,157	9.4
1971	13,534	952	7.0
1972	17,218	1,687	9.8
1973	26,150	3,066	11.7
1974	43,829	4,384	10.0
1975	49,468	3,306	6.7
1976	57,787	4,010	6.9
1977	66,743	5,480	8.2
1978	80,594	6,532	8.1
1979	102,279	7,608	7.4
1980	149,506	10,701	7.2

a. Includes metallurgy.
Source: Central Bank.

Table SA.2. *Share of Mining in Total Labor Force, 1970–81*
(thousands)

Year	Total labor force	Mining labor force[a]	Mining labor force as a percentage of total
1970	1,330	69	5.2
1971	1,359	70	5.2
1972	1,388	72	5.2
1973	1,418	74	5.2
1974	1,448	76	5.2
1975	1,479	73	4.9
1976	1,547	74	4.8
1977	1,589	74	4.7
1978	1,629	78	4.8
1979	1,677	83	4.9
1980	1,720	84	4.9
1981	1,754	80	4.6

a. Excludes metallurgy.
Sources: National Institute of Statistics (INE); Ministry of Labor.

Table SA.3. *Contribution of Mining to Fiscal Revenues, 1970–81*
(millions of U.S. dollars)

Year	Direct contribution of mining sector	Current revenues of central government	Share of mining in current revenues
1970	50.3	73.9	68.1
1971	23.1	64.1	36.0
1972	30.6	77.6	39.4
1973	42.2	123.5	34.2
1974	85.8	253.5	33.8
1975	61.2	284.4	21.5
1976	71.5	342.0	20.9
1977	103.0	382.1	27.0
1978	118.9	427.0	27.8
1979	139.5	412.8	33.8
1980	117.5	481.1	24.4
1981	93.4	566.5	16.5

Sources: Ministry of Finance; Ministry of Mining and Metallurgy; Central Bank.

Table SA.4. *Share of Mining in Total Merchandise Exports, 1970–82*
(millions of U.S. dollars)

Year	Mining exports (c.i.f.)	Total merchandise exports (c.i.f.)	Mining exports as a percentage of total
1970	204.9	228.8	89.6
1971	173.3	216.0	80.2
1972	174.1	240.4	72.4
1973	225.9	338.3	66.8
1974	387.3	650.5	59.5
1975	314.2	536.1	58.6
1976	393.5	649.6	60.6
1977	491.4	719.3	68.3
1978	515.0	723.7	71.2
1979	591.7	859.4	68.8
1980	641.2	1,035.9	61.9
1981	556.0	995.3	55.9
1982	419.3	898.2	46.7

Source: Central Bank.

Table SA.5. *Share of Subsectors in Mining Labor Force, 1970–81*
(thousands)

Year	COMIBOL	Medium mines	Small mines and corporations	Total
1970	21.9	6.3	40.5	68.7
1971	23.0	6.2	40.8	70.0
1972	23.8	5.4	42.7	71.9
1973	24.1	6.0	43.6	73.7
1974	24.6	7.5	43.5	75.6
1975	25.6	7.4	40.4	73.4
1976	24.6	8.5	41.0	74.1
1977	24.6	8.5	41.1	74.2
1978	25.1	7.6	45.6	78.3
1979	26.4	7.7	49.4	83.5
1980	26.5	7.4	49.8	83.7
1981	25.7	7.5	47.2	80.4

Source: Ministry of Mining and Metallurgy.

Table SA.6. *Employment in COMIBOL Mines, 1982*

Name	Underground	Concentrator	Surface	Education and health	Total	Underground as a percentage of total
Catavi	1,352	894	1,442	779	4,467	30.3
Quechisla	1,872	612	1,398	671	4,553	41.1
Colquiri	1,000	393	718	346	2,457	40.7
Huanuni	982	361	458	316	2,117	46.4
Unificada	837	315	564	189	1,905	43.9
San Jose	626	306	464	320	1,716	36.5
Caacoles	589	123	277	138	1,127	52.3
Santa Fe	353	167	251	130	901	39.1
Coroco	465	68	312	108	953	48.8
Viloco	298	101	222	105	726	41.0
Bolivar	258	75	139	58	530	48.7
Colquechaca	167	60	101	32	360	46.4
Matilde	312	47	189	68	616	50.6
Colavi	215	0	118	32	365	58.9
Total	9,326	3,522	6,653	3,292	22,793[a]	40.92

a. Does not include about 3,000 employees working away from mines.
Source: COMIBOL.

Table SA.7. *Composition of Mining Sector Revenues, 1970–81*
(millions of U.S. dollars)

Year	Regalia	Export tax	Others[a]	Total
1970	38.6	0.0	11.7	50.3
1971	15.3	0.0	7.8	23.1
1972	14.9	7.7	8.0	30.6
1973	19.6	15.8	6.8	42.2
1974	44.1	24.0	17.7	85.8
1975	40.5	16.4	4.3	61.2
1976	49.9	16.3	5.3	71.5
1977	74.9	18.8	9.3	103.0
1978	91.5	26.6	0.8	118.9
1979	115.6	22.3	1.6	139.5
1980	115.0	1.3	1.2	117.5
1981	92.7	0.0	0.6	93.3

a. Includes import duties and internal revenue.
Sources: Ministry of Finance; Ministry of Mining and Metallurgy.

Table SA.8. *Source of Regalia Payments, 1970–80*
(millions of U.S. dollars)

Year	COMIBOL	Medium mines	Small mines	Total[a]
1970	9.4	10.0	7.2	26.6
1971	6.3	3.2	2.4	11.9
1972	7.6	2.8	2.2	12.6
1973	13.2	7.9	2.5	24.6
1974	32.7	13.2	9.8	55.7
1975	25.3	11.7	3.4	40.4
1976	28.6	14.7	5.4	48.7
1977	62.9	20.6	8.0	91.5
1978	70.7	23.2	9.8	103.7
1979	78.2	31.2	11.8	121.2
1980	81.4	24.9	12.6	118.9
1981	72.3	11.7	7.1	91.1

Note: Starting in 1975, includes regalias paid by ENAF to the Treasury.
a. This table differs from Tables SA. 4 and SA. 7 because totals in this table are gross, that is, they include earmarked regalias and reductions of regalia payments on excess production.
Sources: Ministry of Finance; Central Bank; Ministry of Mining and Metallurgy.

Table SA.9. *Source of Tin Regalia Payments, 1970–81*
(millions of U.S. dollars)

Year	COMIBOL	Medium-size mines	Small mines	Total
1970	6.3	2.3	1.4	10.0
1971	4.6	1.5	1.5	7.6
1972	6.5	1.4	1.4	9.3
1973	10.3	4.1	1.8	16.2
1974	25.6	6.0	5.5	37.1
1975	19.5	7.2	1.8	28.7
1976	21.5	7.9	2.4	31.8
1977	54.9	13.6	4.6	73.1
1978	64.8	16.6	8.0	89.4
1979	69.0	17.9	9.1	96.0
1980	70.2	19.6	7.1	96.9
1981	68.4	8.0	4.7	81.1

Sources: Ministry of Finance; Central Bank.

Table SA.10. *Source of Export Tax Payments, 1970–80*
(millions of U.S. dollars)

Year	COMIBOL	Medium-size mines	Small mines	ENAF	Total
1970	0.0	0.0	0.0	0.0	0.0
1971	0.0	0.0	0.0	0.0	0.0
1972	5.7	0.0	2.0	0.0	7.7
1973	8.9	2.8	2.8	1.3	15.8
1974	14.1	4.8	2.2	2.9	24.0
1975	8.7	3.2	1.2	3.3	16.4
1976	8.3	3.7	2.0	2.3	16.3
1977	9.8	3.8	1.2	4.0	18.8
1978	9.5	3.2	0.1	13.8	26.6
1979	0.3	3.9	0.3	17.8	22.3
1980	0.0	0.6	0.0	0.7	1.3

Note: The export tax was imposed in 1972 and eliminated in mid-1980.

Table SA.11. *Production of Tin Concentrates, 1973–82*
(fine metric tons)

Year	COMIBOL	Medium-size mines	Small mines and corporations	Total
1973	20,846	7,000	3,582	31,428
1974	20,061	6,940	3,396	30,397
1975	21,438	6,899	4,781	33,118
1976	20,592	6,675	3,100	30,367
1977	23,298	6,833	3,656	33,787
1978	21,471	6,625	2,813	30,909
1979	19,009	5,937	2,812	27,758
1980	18,621	5,880	2,270	26,771
1981	18,639	6,335	2,638	27,612
1982	17,910	6,026	2,836	26,772

Sources: Ministry of Mining and Metallurgy; National Institute of Statistics.

Table SA.12. *Production of Metallic Tin, 1970–82*
(fine metric tons)

Year	ENAF	Funestaño	Total
1970	0.0	0.0	0.0
1971	6,969	0.0	6,969
1972	6,227	0.0	6,227
1973	6,954	0.0	6,954
1974	7,092	36	7,128
1975	7,430	156	7,586
1976	9,185	915	10,100
1977	12,786	439	13,225
1978	16,184	8	16,192
1979	15,696	0.0	15,696
1980	17,863	0.0	17,863
1981	19,860	0.0	19,860
1982	19,463	0.0	19,463

Source: Ministry of Mining and Metallurgy.

Table SA.13. *Bolivian and World Production of Tin Concentrates, 1900–82*
(fine metric tons)

Year	Bolivian production	World production	Bolivian production as a percentage of world production
1900	9,738	86,800	11.2
1901	13,124	90,571	14.5
1902	10,604	85,431	12.4
1903	12,533	91,948	13.6
1904	12,902	93,264	13.8
1905	16,582	95,950	17.3
1906	17,624	98,354	17.9
1907	16,607	99,597	16.7
1908	17,696	105,689	16.7
1909	21,340	112,857	18.9
1910	23,129	111,829	20.7
1911	22,434	113,126	19.8
1912	23,027	118,374	19.5
1913	26,355	127,807	20.6
1914	22,355	119,132	18.8
1915	21,794	122,027	17.9
1916	21,145	120,776	17.5
1917	27,858	120,774	23.1
1918	29,280	117,826	24.9
1919	27,389	114,968	23.8
1920	29,542	113,876	25.9
1921	28,957	111,491	26.0
1922	28,129	115,663	24.3
1923	31,128	119,755	26.0
1924	32,059	136,952	23.4
1925	32,741	139,644	23.4
1926	30,543	139,086	22.0
1927	36,384	155,231	23.4
1928	42,068	173,485	24.2
1929	47,082	192,182	24.5
1930	38,758	176,026	22.0
1931	31,235	140,200	22.2
1932	20,913	93,500	22.4
1933	14,961	81,300	18.4
1934	20,965	113,800	18.4
1935	27,604	140,214	19.7
1936	24,460	183,905	13.3
1937	25,531	209,814	12.2
1938	25,896	167,648	15.4
1939	27,917	170,188	16.4
1940	38,531	238,771	16.1
1941	42,740	249,948	17.1
1942	38,908	122,942	31.6
1943	40,960	141,231	29.0
1944	39,341	101,605	38.7
1945	43,168	89,412	48.3
1946	38,222	90,428	42.3
1947	33,800	114,305	29.6
1948	37,935	153,931	24.6
1949	34,662	164,092	21.1

(Table continues on the following page.)

Table SA.13   (continued).

Year	Bolivian production	World production	Bolivian production as a percentage of world production
1950	31,714	169,172	18.7
1951	22,664	170,188	19.8
1952	32,472	173,744	18.7
1953	35,384	172,830	20.5
1954	29,287	171,712	17.0
1955	28,369	170,696	16.6
1956	27,273	169,070	16.1
1957	28,242	165,717	17.0
1958	18,014	117,658	15.3
1959	24,193	121,113	20.0
1960	19,718	138,690	14.2
1961	20,996	138,800	15.1
1962	22,150	141,900	15.6
1963	22,603	143,600	15.7
1964	24,587	149,300	16.5
1965	23,407	155,100	15.1
1966	25,932	169,800	15.3
1967	27,721	174,800	15.9
1968	29,568	183,200	16.1
1969	30,047	178,900	16.8
1970	29,379	186,300	15.8
1971	30,290	188,100	16.1
1972	32,405	196,300	16.5
1973	31,428	189,100	16.6
1974	30,397	183,600	16.6
1975	33,118	181,200	18.3
1976	30,367	180,000	16.9
1977	33,787	188,400	17.9
1978	30,909	196,600	15.7
1979	27,758	200,400	13.9
1980	26,771	200,100	13.4
1981	27,612	204,700	13.5
1982	26,772	188,900	14.2

Sources: Ministry of Mining and Metallurgy, International Tin Council.

Table SA.14. *Export Values of Tin Concentrates, 1970–82*
(millions of U.S. dollars)

Year	COMIBOL	Medium-size mines	Small mines and corporations	Total
1970	64.4	23.3	14.3	102.0
1971	51.5	17.4	13.1	82.0
1972	59.2	16.5	13.2	88.9
1973	67.3	19.3	12.1	98.7
1974	121.2	28.0	25.3	174.5
1975	98.2	20.3	11.3	129.8
1976	113.0	20.3	20.5	153.8
1977	134.6	21.4	36.9	192.9
1978	117.0	23.1	32.6	172.7
1979	95.6	26.8	43.5	167.6
1980	83.7	15.2	40.4	139.3
1981	32.8	11.8	32.6	77.2
1982	20.2	8.9	11.9	41.0

Source: Ministry of Mining and Metallurgy.

Table SA.15. *Export Values of Metallic Tin, 1970–82*
(millions of U.S. dollars)

Year	ENAF	Funestaño	Total
1970	0.0	0.0	0.0
1971	23.9	0.0	23.9
1972	23.5	1.1	24.6
1973	32.3	0.0	32.3
1974	55.4	0.2	55.6
1975	49.5	0.7	50.2
1976	69.3	5.0	74.3
1977	131.8	4.1	135.9
1978	200.9	0.1	201.0
1979	228.0	0.0	228.0
1980	238.8	0.0	238.8
1981	265.9	0.0	265.9
1982	237.3	0.0	237.3

n.a. Not applicable.
Source: Ministry of Mining and Metallurgy.

Table SA.16. *Sales of Tin Concentrates to ENAF, 1973–81*

| | Fine metric tons | | | As a percentage of total production of each | | |
Year	COMIBOL	Medium-size mines	Small mines and corporations	COMIBOL	Medium-size mines	Small mines and corporations
1973	5,561	2,210	316	26.7	31.6	8.8
1974	4,923	2,692	81	24.5	38.8	2.4
1975	4,607	3,112	211	21.5	45.1	5.5
1976	5,984	4,107	43	29.1	61.5	1.4
1977	10,021	4,051	422	43.0	59.3	11.5
1978	11,760	3,771	21	54.8	56.9	0.7
1979	11,922	3,614	1	62.7	61.2	0.0
1980	13,326	4,092	412	71.6	69.6	18.1
1981	14,915	4,266	1,625	80.0	67.3	61.6

Source: Ministry of Mining and Metallurgy.

Table SA.17. *Distribution of Medium-Size Mines by Fixed Assets, 1973–80*

| Total assets (in millions of pesos) | Number of firms | | | | | | | |
	1973	1974	1975	1976	1977	1978	1979	1980
0 – 0.9	1	2	1	0	3	0	0	0
1 – 4.9	6	5	4	6	3	2	1	1
5 – 19.9	8	9	9	11	11	8	7	3
20 – 39.9	2	5	5	5	5	7	4	6
40 – 99.9	0	0	1	2	2	4	7	6
100 – 149.9	1	2	2	3	2	2	2	2
150 – 199.9	2	1	2	1	1	0	0	1
200 and above	0	0	0	1	2	3	3	5
Total number of firms	20	24	24	29	29	26	24	24
Total assets, all firms (millions of pesos)	708.2	634.7	879.1	1,270.8	1,398.9	1,866.1	2,150.7	2,888.7
Average per firm (millions of pesos)	35.4	26.5	36.6	43.8	48.2	71.8	89.6	120.4

Source: Ministry of Mining and Metallurgy.

Table SA.18. *Distribution of Medium-Size Mines by Total Sales, 1973–80*

| Total sales (in millions of pesos) | Number of firms | | | | | | | |
	1973	1974	1975	1976	1977	1978	1979	1980
Less than 10	5	6	6	6	6	2	2	2
10 – 39.9	9	9	8	13	11	10	8	6
40 – 79.9	2	5	4	3	6	6	3	3
80 – 119.9	2	2	1	1	2	2	3	4
120 – 199.9	1	0	1	2	1	1	3	2
200 – 299.9	1	1	2	2	0	2	2	4
300 and above	0	1	1	1	3	3	3	3
Total sales	20	24	23	28	29	26	24	24
Total sales (millions of pesos)	1,006.2	1,259.2	1,520.5	1,770.7	2,259.1	2,600.4	3,892.7	4,015.6
Average sales (millions of pesos)	50.3	52.5	66.1	63.2	77.9	100.0	162.2	167.3

Source: Ministry of Mining and Metallurgy.

Table SA.19. *Distribution of Medium-Size Mines by Profits, 1973–80*

Firms' reported profits	Number of firms							
(in millions of pesos)	1973	1974	1975	1976	1977	1978	1979	1980
Less than 0	2	1	4	9	10	8	13	11
0 – 0.49	2	2	5	1	5	4	2	3
0.5 – 0.99	4	1	1	1	0	1	1	0
1.0 – 4.99	8	11	9	11	6	4	1	1
5.0 – 9.99	1	2	2	0	2	2	4	2
10.0 – 19.99	1	2	2	0	2	2	4	2
20.0 – 39.99	1	2	0	1	3	2	1	3
40.0 – 79.99	1	2	0	0	1	0	1	1
80 and above	0	0	0	2	1	1	0	1
Total number of firms	20	23	22	29	29	26	24	24
Total profits (millions of pesos)	120.7	244.5	35.3	310.3	165.9	86.7	81.6	270.9
Average profits (millions of pesos)	6.04	10.63	1.60	10.70	5.70	3.30	3.40	11.3

Note: Profits are after taxes.
Source: Ministry of Mining and Metallurgy.

Table SA.20. *Distribution of Medium-Size Mines by Employment, 1974–80*

Number of employees	Number of firms						
	1974	1975	1976	1977	1978	1979	1980
0 – 99	2	3	7	7	2	5	3
100 – 199	9	10	8	8	6	4	6
200 – 299	7	6	7	8	9	7	8
300 – 499	1	1	2	3	4	5	4
500 – 699	1	3	3	0	0	0	0
700 – 899	4	0	0	0	0	0	0
900 and above	0	2	2	3	3	3	3
Total number of firms	24	25	29	29	24	24	24
Total employment	7,476	7,456	8,480	8,516	7,640	7,740	7,400
Average employment per firm	311	298	292	294	336	322	326

Source: Ministry of Mining and Metallurgy.

Table SA.21. *World Production of Tin Concentrates, 1900–81*

(thousands of tons of tin)

Region and country	1900	1930	1950	1960	1970	1975	1981
Latin America							
Bolivia	9.7	38.8	31.7	19.7	29.4	33.1	27.6
Brazil	0.0	0.0	0.0	1.6	3.7	5.0	8.3
Others	0.0	0.3	0.7	0.6	2.8	0.9	1.7
Subtotal	9.7	39.1	32.4	21.9	35.9	39.0	37.6
Southeast Asia and Australia							
Malaysia	43.8	68.0	58.7	52.8	75.0	64.4	60.0
Thailand	3.9	11.2	10.5	12.3	22.1	16.4	31.5
Indonesia	17.9	35.5	32.6	23.0	19.4	25.3	35.3
Australia	4.4	1.5	1.9	2.2	9.0	9.3	12.9
Others	0.1	5.0	1.8	1.4	0.9	1.3	2.0
Subtotal	70.1	121.2	105.5	91.7	126.4	116.7	141.7
Africa							
Nigeria	0.0	8.8	8.4	7.8	8.1	4.7	2.5
Zaire	0.0	0.7	11.9	9.4	6.6	4.6	2.4
South Africa	0.0	0.9	0.7	0.7	1.5	2.8	2.4
Others	0.0	0.0	1.7	2.7	3.1	4.1	3.6
Subtotal	0.0	10.4	22.7	20.6	19.3	16.2	10.9
Others							
United Kingdom	4.3	2.5	0.9	1.2	1.8	3.3	3.9
Others	0.1	0.8	2.1	2.2	5.9	2.6	2.1
Subtotal	4.4	3.3	3.0	3.4	7.7	5.9	6.0
World[a]	84.2	174.0	163.6	137.6	189.3	177.8	196.2

a. Excluding Albania, China, the German Democratic Republic, the Peoples' Republic of Korea, U.S.S.R., and Vietnam.
Sources: For 1900, 1938, and 1950, C. J. Schmitz, *World Non-Ferrous Metal Production and Prices, 1700-1976* (N.J.: Totowa, Biblio Dist., 1979); International Tin Council, *Tin Statistics* (various issues) for 1960 on.

Table SA.22. *Rank of Major Producing Countries with Respect to Production of Tin Concentrates, 1960–82*

Country	1960	1961–62	1963	1964	1965–72	1973–76	1978	1979–80	1981–82
Malaysia	1	1	1	1	1	1	1	1	1
Indonesia	2	3	4	3	4	3	4	3	2
Thailand	4	4	3	4	3	4	3	2	3
Bolivia	3	2	2	2	2	2	2	4	4

Source: International Tin Council.

Table SA.23. *Production of Tin Metal*
(thousands of tons)

Country	1900	1930	1950	1960	1970	1975	1981
Ore-producing countries							
Latin America							
Bolivia	0.0	0.0	0.0	1.0	0.3	7.6	19.9
Brazil	0.0	0.0	0.1	1.3	3.1	5.4	7.6
Others[a]	0.0	0.0	0.3	1.3	1.1	1.1	0.9
Subtotal	0.0	0.0	0.4	3.6	4.5	14.1	28.4
Southeast Asia and Australia							
Malaysia	0.0	98.3	69.9	77.6	91.5	64.4	60.0
Thailand	0.0	0.0	0.0	0.2	22.0	16.4	31.5
Indonesia	0.0	14.9	0.4	2.0	5.2	25.3	35.3
Australia	0.0	1.6	2.0	2.3	5.2	9.3	12.9
Others[b]	0.0	0.0	0.0	0.0	0.0	1.3	2.0
Subtotal	0.0	114.8	72.3	82.1	123.9	116.7	141.7
Africa							
Nigeria	0.0	0.0	0.0	0.0	8.1	4.7	2.5
Zaire	0.0	0.0	3.3	2.5	1.4	4.6	2.4
South Africa	0.0	0.0	0.7	0.7	1.5	2.8	2.4
Others[c]	0.0	0.0	0.0	0.6	0.6	4.1	3.6
Subtotal	0.0	0.0	4.0	3.8	11.6	16.2	10.9
Subtotal	0.0	114.8	76.7	89.5	140.0	145.0	178.2
Nonore-producing countries							
United Kingdom[d]	7.9	51.4	29.0	28.8	22.0	11.6	6.9
Others[e]	71.4	14.8	81.3	31.7	21.7	19.2	11.7
Subtotal	79.3	66.2	110.3	60.5	43.7	30.8	18.6
World[f]	79.3	181.0	187.0	150.0	183.7	176.3	196.9

Note: Tin metal refers to primary tin only.

a. Peru and Mexico.

b. Includes Singapore, whose metal production relies on ore produced in its vicinity.

c. Zimbabwe.

d. Although the United Kingdom is one of the major ore producers, it is classified as a nonore-producing country because its metal production relies heavily on imported ores.

e. Including countries that produce less than 1,000 tons of ores a year, such as Spain, Portugal, Japan, the Republic of Korea, Canada, and the United States.

f. Excludes Albania, China, the German Democratic Republic, the Peoples' Republic of Korea, the U.S.S.R., and Vietnam.

Sources: For 1900, 1938, and 1950; C. J. Schmitz, *World Non-Ferrous Metal Production and Price, 1700-1976*; International Tin Council, *Tin Statistics* (various issues) for 1960 on.

Table SA.24. *Percentage Shares of Production by Economic Group, 1980*

(percent)

Production	Industrial economies	Developing economies	Centrally planned economies
Ore production			
Tin	6.9	84.8	8.3
Bauxite	33.1	56.0	10.9
Copper	30.0	49.9	20.1
Lead	45.2	33.3	21.5
Zinc	50.5	27.5	22.0
Iron ore	33.8	37.5	28.7
Metal production			
Tin	9.7	82.2	8.1
Aluminum	65.6	16.3	18.1
Copper	49.8	28.5	21.7
Lead	60.2	19.3	20.5
Zinc	56.8	19.4	23.8
Steel	54.7	15.6	29.3

Source: The World Bank.

Table SA.25. *Consumption of Tin Metal, 1950–81*

(thousands of tons)

Region or country	1950	1960	1970	1975	1981
Ore-producing region					
Latin America[a]	3.1	5.0	6.6	8.9	7.7
Asia and Oceania[b]	3.1	5.5	6.1	5.8	6.0
Africa[c]	1.9	3.1	2.8	3.3	2.4
Subtotal	8.1	13.6	15.5	18.0	16.1
Nonore-producing countries					
United States and Canada	76.9	56.3	58.4	47.9	44.3
European Community-9	48.7	69.8	58.4	49.8	41.7
Other western European countries	5.7	6.4	8.5	10.3	8.2
Japan and East Asia	4.7	13.4	25.9	29.9	34.9
Others	5.0	4.8	5.5	3.9	3.6
CPEs[d]	3.9	4.3	11.3	13.0	10.8
Subtotal	144.9	154.6	168.0	154.8	143.5
World	153.0	168.2	183.5	172.8	159.6

a. Brazil, Bolivia, Peru, and Mexico.

b. Malaysia, Thailand, Indonesia, Australia, and Singapore.

c. Nigeria, Zaire, South Africa, and Zimbabwe.

d. Excluding Albania, China, the German Democratic Republic, the People's Republic of Korea, Mongolia, U.S.S.R., and Vietnam.

Source: International Tin Council, *Tin Statistics* (various issues).

Table SA.26. *Annual Growth Rate of Tin Consumption by Product and Country, 1963–81*

Product	United States	United Kingdom	Federal Republic of Germany	France	EC[a]	Japan	All reporting countries[b]
Tin plate	−4.3	−4.8	1.4	−0.8	−0.2	2.9	−1.6
Tinning	0.2	−3.2	−7.7	−5.5	−5.2	4.8	−1.1
Solder	−1.0	−4.3	4.6	0.2	0.4	4.6	0.5
White metal, babbitt and anti-friction metal	−0.9	−2.6	11.6	1.9	−1.2	−2.8	0.6
Bronze and brass	−4.4	−4.2	1.6	−2.8	−3.3	−0.8	−4.1
Others	4.5	−1.2	1.8	−0.1	1.0	10.7	0.2
Total	−1.8	−3.8	1.9	−0.7	−1.0	0.4	−0.7

a. The United Kingdom, the Federal Republic of Germany, and France.
b. Includes the countries listed, plus Belgium, Italy, the Netherlands, Switzerland, Austria, and Australia.
Source: The World Bank.

Table SA.27. *Trade Flows of Tin Concentrates, 1965*
(tons of tin)

Exporting country	Importing country							
	United States and Canada	Western Europe	Japan and East Asia	Southeast Asia, China, and Australia	Latin America	CPEs[a]	Others	Total
Bolivia	7,552	16,643	0	0	0	0	15	24,210
Other Latin American countries	0	0	0	0	0	0	0	0
Southeast Asia, China, and Australia	0	664	0	22	0	0	0	686
Africa	0	4,988	0	0	0	0	28	5,016
United States and Canada	49	65	0	0	106	0	0	220
Western Europe	0	0	0	0	0	0	0	0
Total	7,601	22,360	0	22	106	0	43	30,132

a. Centrally planned economies.
Source: International Tin Council, *Tin Statistics, 1965–75.*

Table SA.28. *Trade Flows of Tin Metal, 1965*
(tons)

Exporting country	United States and Canada	Western Europe	Japan and East Asia	Southeast Asia, China, and Australia	Latin America	CPEs[a]	Others	Total
Bolivia	425	0	0	0	0	0	3,045	3,470
Other Latin American countries	0	0	0	0	0	0	0	0
Southeast Asia, China, and Australia	38,619	18,222	15,258	2,123	1,481	3,287	8,089	87,079
Africa	1,682	10,230	0	0	0	127	152	12,191
United States and Canada	337	112	61	0	672	0	1,695	2,877
Western Europe	1,532	20,040	0	0	0	3,374	2,773	27,719
Total	42,595	48,604	15,319	2,123	2,153	6,788	15,754	133,336

a. Centrally planned economies.
Source: International Tin Council, *Tin Statistics, 1965–75.*

Table SA.29. *Trade Flows of Tin Concentrates, 1970*
(tons of tin)

Exporting country	Importing country							
	United States and Canada	Western Europe	Japan and East Asia	Southeast Asia, China, and Australia	Latin America	CPEs[a]	Others	Total
Bolivia	3,561	23,675	0	0	76	525	1,542	29,379
Other Latin American countries	0	0	0	0	0	0	0	0
Southeast Asia, China, and Australia	0	2,965	0	14,803	27	0	812	18,607
Africa	0	7,385	0	0	0	0	228	7,613
United States and Canada	79	0	0	0	184	0	5	268
Western Europe	0	590	0	0	0	0	0	590
Total	3,640	34,615	0	14,803	287	525	2,587	56,457

a. Centrally planned economies.
Source: International Tin Council, *Tin Statistics, 1970–80.*

Table SA.30. *Trade Flows of Tin Metal, 1970*

(tons)

Exporting country	Importing country							
	United States and Canada	Western Europe	Japan and East Asia	Southeast Asia, China, and Australia	Latin America	CPEs[a]	Others	Total
Bolivia	0	0	0	0	0	302	0	302
Other Latin American countries	396	0	0	0	0	0	0	396
Southeast Asia, China, and Australia	52,283	33,972	27,811	973	1,128	5,330	3,454	124,951
Africa	930	9,605	0	0	0	111	1,752	12,398
United States and Canada	503	80	0	0	298	0	3,643	4,524
Western Europe	698	11,965	0	0	27	8,454	850	21,994
Total	54,810	55,622	27,811	973	1,453	14,197	9,699	164,565

a. Centrally planned economies.
Source: International Tin Council, *Tin Statistics, 1970–80.*

Table SA.31. *Trade Flows of Tin Concentrates, 1975*
(tons)

Exporting country	Importing country							
	United States and Canada	Western Europe	Japan and East Asia	Southeast Asia, China, and Australia	Latin America	CPEs[a]	Others	Total
Bolivia	6,841	10,222	0	0	1,242	616	23	18,944
Other Latin American countries	0	0	0	0	0	0	0	0
Southeast Asia, China, and Australia	0	1,867	83	15,527	450	592	198	18,717
Africa	0	7,206	0	111	0	0	0	7,317
United States and Canada	801	165	6	0	52	0	34	1,052
Western Europe	0	315	0	0	0	0	128	443
Total	7,642	19,775	83	15,638	1,744	1,208	383	46,473

a. Centrally planned economies.
Source: International Tin Council, *Tin Statistics, 1970–80.*

Table SA.32. *Trade Flows of Tin Metal, 1975*
(tons)

Exporting country	United States and Canada	Western Europe	Japan and East Asia	Importing country Southeast Asia, China, and Australia	Latin America	CPEs[a]	Others	Total
Bolivia	611	2,248	0	0	914	3,365	360	7,498
Other Latin American countries	1,230	1,230	0	0	1,029	0	29	3,491
Southeast Asia, China, and Australia	41,135	43,087	22,414	644	5	9,453	4,305	121,093
Africa	0	5,577	0	0	0	0	105	5,682
United States and Canada	998	1,452	0	0	983	0	163	3,596
Western Europe	516	7,752	0	0	45	652	1,152	10,117
Total	44,490	61,319	22,414	644	2,976	13,470	6,114	151,427

a. Centrally planned economies.
Source: International Tin Council, *Tin Statistics, 1970–80.*

Table SA.33. *Trade Flows of Tin Concentrates, 1981*
(tons of tin)

				Importing country				
Exporting country	United States and Canada	Western Europe	Japan and East Asia	Southeast Asia, China, and Australia	Latin America	CPEs[a]	Others	Total
Bolivia	20	3,910	0	0	0	730	860	5,520
Other Latin American countries	0	0	0	0	0	0	0	0
Southeast Asia, China, and Australia	0	1,520	16	8,572	607	293	330	11,338
Africa	0	2,204	0	40	0	0	794	3,038
United States and Canada	0	830	0	156	0	0	68	1,054
Western Europe	383	63	0	0	67	0	0	513
Total	403	8,527	16	8,768	674	1,023	2,052	21,463

a. Centrally planned economies.
Source: International Tin Council, *Tin Statistics, 1971–81.*

Table SA.34. *Trade Flows of Tin Metal, 1981*
(tons)

Exporting country	Importing country							
	United States and Canada	Western Europe	Japan and East Asia	Southeast Asia, China, and Australia	Latin America	CPEs[a]	Others	Total
Bolivia	10,910	4,701	0	0	399	908	1,034	17,952
Other Latin American countries	1,156	2,389	0	0	1,521	480	0	5,946
Southeast Asia, China, and Australia	30,673	57,257	33,881	13,408	48	7,429	8,645	151,338
Africa	520	2,176	0	0	0	0	15	2,711
United States and Canada	2,626	1,931	6	0	676	0	841	6,080
Western Europe	108	6,408	0	0	194	5,191	817	12,718
Total	46,393	74,862	33,887	13,408	2,835	14,008	11,352	196,745

a. Centrally planned economies.
Source: International Tin Council, *Tin Statistics, 1971–81.*

103

Table SA.35. *Relative Prices of Tin with Respect to Other Major Metals, 1800–1982*

Period	Aluminum	Copper	Lead	Zinc
1800[a]	0.0	0.7	5.2	0.0
1850[a]	0.0	1.0	4.9	5.2
1900[a]	0.8	1.0	8.7	6.2
1930[a]	1.7	2.4	8.6	8.7
1950–54	6.1	3.7	7.2	7.1
1955–59	4.2	3.0	8.2	9.1
1960–64	5.1	3.7	13.2	11.0
1965–69	6.3	2.6	12.9	12.2
1970–74	6.8	3.2	12.8	7.8
1975–79	10.4	7.3	16.0	15.9
1980–82	10.6	8.2	20.7	17.4

Note: The price of the metal with which the tin price is compared is set at 1.00.
a. Based on the three-year-average price.
Sources: Schmitz, *World Non-Ferrous Metal Production and Prices*, for 1800–1930; and World Bank data for the others.

Table SA.36. *Price Indices of Tin, Aluminum, and Copper, 1950–82*

Period	Tin[a]	Aluminum[b]	Copper[c]
1950–54	1.01	0.86	1.00
1955–59	0.84	1.04	1.09
1960–64	1.00	1.00	1.00
1965–69	1.27	1.03	1.78
1970–74	1.22	0.92	1.40
1975–79	1.48	0.73	0.75
1980–82	1.60	0.78	0.72

Note: Based on prices in 1980 constant U.S. dollars, the deflator being the World Bank's unit value index of manufactured exports from developed to developing countries on a c.i.f. basis; the five-year average shown in each period group is based on having 1960–64 = 1.00.
a. London Metal Exchange, standard minimum 99.75 percent, settlement price.
b. London Market, 99.0–99.5 percent ingot, spot price.
c. London Metal Market Exchange, electrolytic wirebar, settlement price.
Source: The World Bank.

BIBLIOGRAPHY

Alexander, Robert J. *Bolivia: Past, Present and Future of Its Politics*. New York Praeger, 1968.

Almaraz Paz, Sergio. *Requiem Para Una República*. La Paz: Universidad Mayor de San Andres, 1969.

Almaraz Paz, Sergio. *El Poder y La Caida*. La Paz: Editorial Los Amigos del Libro, 1980.

Anstee, Margaret J. *Gate of the Sun: A Prospect of Bolivia*. London: Longman, 1970.

Baptista Gumucio, Fernando. *Estrategia Nacional Para El Hierro y El Acero*. La Paz: Los Amigos del Libro, 1982.

Bedregal G., Guillermo. *La Nacionalización Minera y La Responsabilidad del Sindicalismo*. La Paz, 1959.

Bohan, Merwin L. *Report of the U.S. Economic Mission to Bolivia*. La Paz: U.S. Economic Mission, 1942.

Bosson, Rex, and Bension Varon. *The Mining Industry and the Developing Countries*. New York: Oxford University Press, 1977.

Canelas Orellana, Amado. *Nacionalización de las Minas de Bolivia: Historia de Una Frustración*. La Paz: Libreria Altiplano, 1963.

———. *Mito y Realidad de la Corporación Minera de Bolivia*. La Paz: Editorial Los Amigos del Libro, 1969.

———. *Quiebra de la Mineria Estatal Boliviana?* La Paz: Editorial Los Amigos del Libro, 1981.

Choksi, Armeane M. *State Intervention in the Industrialization of Developing Countries: Selected Issues*. Washington, D.C.: World Bank Staff Working Paper no. 341, 1979.

Contreras, Manuel. "Tin Mining in Bolivia, 1900–1925." Unpublished M.A. thesis, London University, 1979.

Corporación Minera de Bolivia. *Operación Triangular*. La Paz: Corporación Minera de Bolivia, March 1964.

Crespo, Alfonso. *Los Aramayo de Chicas: Tres Generaciones de Mineros Bolivianos*. Barcelona: Editorial Blume, 1981.

Crespo Rodas, Alberto: "Fundación de la Villa de San Felipe de Austria." *Revista Historica*, vol. 29, 1967.

Eder, George Jackson. *Inflation and Development in Latin America: A Case History of Inflation and Stabilization in Bolivia*. Ann Arbor: University of Michigan, 1968.

Ford, Bacon & Davis, Inc. *The Mining Industry of Bolivia*. La Paz: Ford, Bacon & Davis, 1956.

Fox, David J. "The Bolivian Tin Mining Industry: Some Geographical and Economic Problems." In ITC, *Proceedings of a Technical Conference on Tin*. London, 1967.

Fox, William. *Tin: The Working of a Commodity Agreement*. London: Mining Journal Books Limited, 1974.

Gall, Norman. "Bolivia: The Price of Tin. Part II: The Crisis of Nationalization." *The American Universities Field Staff Report*, vol. 21, no. 2, 1974.

Geddes, C. F. *Patino, the Tin King*. London: Robert Hale, 1972.

Gillis, Malcolm, and others. *Taxation and Mining: Non-fuel Minerals in Bolivia and Other Countries*. Cambridge, Mass.: Ballinger, 1978.

Gomez D'Angelo, Walter. "Mining in the Economic Development of Bolivia," Ph.D. dissertation, Vanderbilt University, 1973.

Hanke, Lewis. *The Imperial City of Potosí*. The Hague: Nijhoff, 1956.

Hashimoto, Hideo. "Modelling Material Substitution in the Tin-Tinplate TFS Complex." World Bank Commodity Division Working Paper. Washington, D.C., 1983.

Hillman, John. "The Nationalized Mining Industry of Bolivia, 1952–1956." 1982.

Ibanez C., Donaciano. *Historia Mineral de Bolivia*. Antofagasta: MacFarlane, 1943.

Jordan Pando, Roberto. *Plan Decenal*. La Paz: Editorial E. Burillo, 1962.

Keenleyside, Hugh. *Report of the United Nations Mission of Technical Assistance to Bolivia*. New York: United Nations, 1951.

Klein, Herbert S. *The Creation of the Patino Tin Empire*, Inter-American Economic Affairs, Autumn, 1965.

———. *Parties and Political Change in Bolivia 1880–1952*. Cambridge, Mass.: Cambridge University Press, 1969.

Ladman, Jerry (ed.). "Modern-Day Bolivia: Legacy of the Revolution and Prospects for the Future." Arizona: Arizona State University, 1982.

Lora, Guillermo. *La Revolución Boliviana*. La Paz: Difusión SRL, 1963.

Malloy, James. *Bolivia: The Uncompleted Revolution*. Pittsburgh, Pa.: Pittsburgh University Press, 1970.

Malloy, James and Richard Thorn (eds.). *Beyond the Revolution: Bolivia Since 1952*. Pittsburgh, Pa.: University of Pittsburgh Press, 1971.

Marsh, Margaret A. *The Bankers in Bolivia: A Study in American Foreign Investment*. New York: AMS Press, 1970.

Mitchell, Christopher. *The Legacy of Populism in Bolivia: From the MNR to Military Rule*. New York: Praeger, 1977.

Muller-Ohlsen, Lotte. *Non-Ferrous Metals: Their Role in Industrial Development*. Cambridge, England: Woodhead-Faulkner in association with Metallgesellschaft AG, 1981.

Muñoz Reues, Jorge. *Geografia de Bolivia*. La Paz: Academia Nacional de Ciencias de Bolivia, 1977.

Musgrave, Richard. "Fiscal Reform in Bolivia." Cambridge, Mass.: Musgrave Mission, 1977.

Nankani, Gobind: *Development Problems of Mineral Exporting Countries*. World Bank Staff Working Paper no. 354, Washington, D.C., 1979.

Nash, June. *We Eat the Mines and the Mines Eat Us: Dependency and Exploitation in Bolivian Tin Mines*. New York: Columbia University Press, 1979.

Ostria Gutierrrez, Alberto: *A People Crucified: The Tragedy of Bolivia*. New York: Prestige Books, 1958.

Patino Mines and Enterprises Consolidated. Annual Report. December 31, 1925.

Penaloza, Luis. *Historia del Movimiento Nacionalista Revolucionario, 1941–1952*. La Paz: Editorial Libreria, 1963.

Pinell-Siles, Armando. "Alternative Strategies for the Economic Development of Bolivia." In *Fiscal Reform in Bolivia*. Cambridge, Mass.: Musgrave Mission, 1977.

Price Waterhouse Associates: "COMIBOL: Diagnostica y Plan de Rehabilitación." A study done for the World Bank/UNDP. 1982.

Querejasu Calvo, Roberto. *Llallagua: Historia de Una Montana*. La Paz: Editorial Los Amigos del Libro, 1977.

Reyes, Simon. *La Masacre de San Juan*. Oruro, 1967.

Robertson, William. *Tin: Its Production and Marketing*. Westport, Conn.:Greenwood Press, 1982.

Ruiz Gonzalez, René. *La Administración Empirica de las Minas Nacionalizadas*. La Paz, 1965.

Shurz, W. L. *Bolivia: A Commercial and Industrial Handbook*.

Thoburn, John. *Multinationals, Mining and Development*. Westmead, Farnborough: Gower Publishing Company, 1981.

Urioste, Armando de. "Asistencia a la Corporación Minera de Bolivia: Un Analisis Crítico de Esfuerzos Pasados y Presentes." Unpublished report for the World Bank. Washington, D.C., March, 1981.

Velasco, S. José Miguel. *Mito y Realidad de las Fundiciones en Bolivia*. La Paz, 1964.

Wilkie, James W. *The Bolivian Revolution and U.S. Aid Since 1952*. Los Angeles: Latin American Center, University of California at Los Angeles, 1969.

Zondag, Cornelius, H. *The Bolivian Economy, 1952–65: The Revolution and Its Aftermath*. New York: Praeger, 1966.

The most recent World Bank publications are described in the annual spring and fall lists; the continuing research program is described in the annual *World Bank Research Program: Abstracts of Current Studies*. The latest edition of each is available free of charge from the Publications Sales Unit, Department B, The World Bank, Washington, D.C. 20433, U.S.A.

Mahmood Ali Ayub, a Pakistani national, was formerly a country economist in the Latin America and Caribbean Regional Office of the World Bank and later served as the Bank's resident representative to Bolivia during 1981–83. He is currently a senior industrial economist in the Industry Department of the Bank.

Hideo Hashimoto, a Japanese national, served as an economist in the Commodity Studies and Projections Division of the Bank. Currently on leave of absence from the Bank, he is serving as the mining advisor to the Ministry of Finance in Ghana.